GOODSON MUMBA

THE HEART OF THE COMPANY

Essential Guide to Organizational Culture

Copyright © 2024 by Goodson Mumba

All rights reserved. No part of this publication may be reproduced, stored or transmitted in any form or by any means, electronic, mechanical, photocopying, recording, scanning, or otherwise without written permission from the publisher. It is illegal to copy this book, post it to a website, or distribute it by any other means without permission.

First edition

ISBN: 9798334952614

This book was professionally typeset on Reedsy. Find out more at reedsy.com

Contents

Preface		iv
Acknowledgement		vi
Dedication		vii
Disclaimer		viii
1	Chapter 1: Understanding Organizational Culture	1
2	Chapter 2: Creating a Vision and Mission	20
3	Chapter 3: Leadership and Culture	37
4	Chapter 4: Employee Engagement and Motivation	52
5	Chapter 5: Communication in Organizational Culture	68
6	Chapter 6: Diversity, Equity, and Inclusion	85
7	Chapter 7: Developing and Sustaining Culture	102
8	Chapter 8: Measuring and Evaluating Culture	121
9	Chapter 9: The Impact of Technology on Culture	138
10	Chapter 10: Case Studies and Best Practices	156
About the Author		171

Preface

In today's fast-paced and ever-evolving business landscape, the importance of a strong and adaptive organizational culture cannot be overstated. "The Heart of the Company: Essential Guide to Organizational Culture" is a comprehensive exploration into the fundamental principles and practices that shape the essence of successful organizations. This book aims to provide leaders, managers, and employees with practical insights and actionable strategies to cultivate a thriving, resilient culture that drives sustained success.

The inspiration for this book stems from my own journey as an infopreneur, thought leader, management consultant, and author. Over the years, I have had the privilege of working with diverse organizations, each with its own unique culture and set of challenges. Through these experiences, I have come to appreciate that the true heart of any company lies in its culture—the collective values, beliefs, and behaviors that define how work is done and how people interact.

Organizational culture is not a static entity; it evolves with time, influenced by internal dynamics and external forces. In this book, we delve into the complexities of culture, examining its roots, its impact on business success, and the role of leadership in shaping and sustaining it. We explore the essential components of a strong culture, including vision and mission, employee engagement, communication, diversity, equity, and inclusion.

Each chapter is designed to provide a deep dive into specific aspects of organizational culture, enriched with real-world case studies and practical examples. From understanding and defining culture to creating a vision and mission, from leadership and communication to the integration of technology, this book offers a holistic approach to building and maintaining a vibrant organizational culture.

Our journey begins with an exploration of the foundational elements of culture, followed by strategies for fostering engagement, communication, and inclusivity. We then move into the critical areas of leadership, measurement, and continuous improvement. By the end of this book, you will have a comprehensive toolkit to help you navigate the challenges and opportunities of cultural transformation within your organization.

I would like to extend my heartfelt gratitude to the numerous organizations, leaders, and employees who have shared their experiences and insights with me. Their stories and lessons form the backbone of this book, providing valuable perspectives that bring the principles of organizational culture to life.

It is my hope that "The Heart of the Company" will serve as a trusted companion on your journey to creating a culture that not only drives business success but also fosters a sense of purpose, belonging, and fulfillment for everyone in your organization.

Thank you for embarking on this journey with me. Together, let us unlock the true potential of our organizations by nurturing the heart of the company—our culture.

Warm regards,

Goodson Mumba

Acknowledgement

I would like to eternally and gratefully acknowledge the Almighty God for the infinite intelligence from His universal mind where we draw from all that we come to know and are yet to know. May I also acknowledge and thank everyone that has played a part in my journey of life in terms of spiritual, moral, emotional and material support.

Dedication

I extend my sincerest gratitude to my beloved wife, Edith Mumba, and our children, Angelina, Lubuto, Letticia, Lulumbi, and Butusho, for their unwavering support and understanding throughout the conception, writing, and eventual publication of this book, despite the sacrifices and challenges they endured.

Disclaimer

This book is a work of fiction. Names, characters, businesses, places, events, and incidents are either the products of the author's imagination or used in a fictitious manner. Any resemblance to actual persons, living or dead, or actual events is purely coincidental.

1

Chapter 1: Understanding Organizational Culture

Defining Organizational Culture

David Lawson sat at his desk in his cozy, book-lined study, sipping his morning coffee as the spring sunlight streamed through the window. His phone rang, breaking the tranquility. Glancing at the caller ID, he saw it was Sarah Mitchell, the CEO of Innovatech. David hadn't spoken to her in years, not since she had taken the helm of the tech giant.

"Good morning, Sarah," David answered, curiosity piqued.

"David, I hope you're doing well," Sarah began, her voice carrying a mix of determination and weariness. "I need your help. Innovatech is in trouble."

David leaned back in his chair, listening intently as Sarah continued.

"Our culture is disintegrating. Employees are disengaged, turnover rates are high, and our innovation has stalled. We've lost our way, David. We need to redefine who we are."

David's mind raced. Innovatech had always been known for its cutting-edge technology and vibrant workplace culture. What had gone wrong?

"I understand, Sarah. Let's start by defining what organizational culture means for Innovatech," David said, grabbing a notebook.

"Yes, that's exactly where we need to start. Can you come in tomorrow?" Sarah asked, hope evident in her voice.

The next morning, David arrived at Innovatech's sleek, modern headquarters. He was greeted by Sarah, who looked both relieved and anxious.

"Thank you for coming, David," she said, leading him to a conference room where the senior leadership team was waiting.

David took a deep breath and began, "To understand what's happening, we first need to define organizational culture. Culture isn't just about perks and benefits; it's the very heart of your organization. It's the values, beliefs, and behaviors that shape how your employees interact and how they work together to achieve your goals."

He walked over to a whiteboard and wrote, "Organizational Culture = Values + Behaviors + Interactions."

"Culture is the invisible glue that holds everything together," he continued. "It's reflected in how decisions are made, how conflict is handled, and how your employees feel about their work and their colleagues."

Sarah nodded, her expression serious. "We used to have a great culture, but it feels like we've lost it."

David turned back to the board. "Let's break it down. What are the core values that Innovatech was founded on? What

CHAPTER 1: UNDERSTANDING ORGANIZATIONAL CULTURE

behaviors do you expect from your employees, and what kind of interactions do you want to promote?"

The team looked around, hesitant at first, but soon began to share their thoughts.

"Collaboration," said Mark, the head of engineering. "We used to be great at working together, but now everyone's in silos."

"Innovation," added Lisa, the marketing director. "We used to take risks, but now we're too focused on playing it safe."

"Respect and inclusivity," said Tom, the HR manager. "We need to bring back a sense of community and support."

David smiled. "These are all excellent points. To rebuild your culture, we need to reinforce these values and make them a part of everyday life at Innovatech."

He handed out a survey to the leadership team. "I want each of you to fill this out, and then we'll distribute it to your teams. It's crucial to get everyone's input to understand their perspectives on what Innovatech's culture is and what it should be."

As the meeting wrapped up, Sarah pulled David aside. "Do you think we can do this, David? Can we really turn things around?"

David looked her in the eye. "It's going to be a challenging journey, Sarah, but yes, I believe you can. The heart of Innovatech is still beating; we just need to find it again and help it thrive."

That evening, back at his study, David reflected on the day's events. He knew this was just the beginning, but he felt a renewed sense of purpose. Helping Innovatech rediscover its heart would not only save the company but also reignite the passion and creativity that had once made it a beacon of innovation.

The History and Evolution of Organizational Culture

David Lawson arrived at Innovatech's headquarters early the next day, ready to dive deeper into the company's cultural issues. He was greeted by Sarah Mitchell, who escorted him to a spacious conference room. The senior leadership team was already assembled, their expressions a mix of anticipation and concern.

"Good morning, everyone," David began, placing his briefcase on the table. "Yesterday, we defined what organizational culture means for Innovatech. Today, we need to explore the history and evolution of organizational culture to understand how we got here."

He clicked a remote, and a projector displayed a timeline on the screen.

"Organizational culture has evolved significantly over the decades," David explained. "In the early 20th century, companies were structured around rigid hierarchies and strict protocols. The focus was on efficiency and productivity, often at the expense of employee well-being."

He pointed to the timeline. "During the 1950s and 60s, we saw the rise of human relations theory, emphasizing the importance of employee satisfaction and motivation. This era introduced the concept that happy employees are more productive."

David glanced around the room, noting the attentive faces. "Then came the 1980s and 90s, the age of corporate culture. Companies like Apple and Google started prioritizing unique workplace cultures to attract and retain top talent. Innovation and creativity became the new currency."

Sarah nodded thoughtfully. "Innovatech was founded during that time. We were known for our vibrant, risk-taking culture."

"Exactly," David replied, highlighting the period on the timeline. "Innovatech was a product of this cultural revolution. You thrived because you embraced innovation and fostered a collaborative, inclusive environment."

David clicked the remote again, revealing a more recent timeline. "In the 2000s and 2010s, globalization and technology further transformed organizational culture. Remote work, digital communication, and diverse, global teams became the norm."

He paused, allowing the team to absorb the information. "However, with these advancements came new challenges. Maintaining a cohesive culture across different locations and time zones, managing rapid technological changes, and addressing the diverse needs of a global workforce became critical."

Mark, the head of engineering, raised his hand. "So, what happened to Innovatech? We were doing so well, and then it all seemed to fall apart."

David nodded. "That's a great question. Innovatech initially rode the wave of these cultural shifts. But over time, as the company grew, you faced difficulties maintaining the core values that made you successful. The rapid expansion, the pressure to perform, and the shift to remote work during the pandemic created strains on your culture."

He turned to Sarah. "Sarah, can you share some insights on the key cultural milestones and challenges Innovatech faced over the years?"

Sarah took a deep breath. "Well, we started as a small,

innovative team with a strong sense of camaraderie. Everyone knew each other, and communication was seamless. As we grew, we hired more people, opened new offices, and expanded our product lines. Somewhere along the way, we lost that close-knit feel. The focus shifted to meeting targets and deadlines, and we neglected our culture."

David nodded. "It's a common story. Growth and success can sometimes lead to cultural dilution if the core values aren't reinforced consistently."

He turned back to the team. "Understanding the history and evolution of organizational culture helps us see where we went wrong and what needs to change. Innovatech needs to reconnect with its roots while adapting to the modern business environment."

David clicked to the final slide, which displayed Innovatech's founding values. "Innovation, collaboration, respect, and inclusivity – these are the values that built Innovatech. We need to reignite these values and integrate them into every aspect of the company."

As the meeting concluded, David handed out a detailed questionnaire to the leadership team. "This survey will help us gather more specific insights from your employees about how they perceive Innovatech's culture, past and present. We'll use this data to craft a plan for moving forward."

Sarah stood up, a determined look in her eyes. "Thank you, David. We have a long road ahead, but I'm confident we can bring back the heart of Innovatech."

David smiled, feeling the weight of the challenge but also the potential for transformation. The journey had just begun, and he was ready to guide Innovatech back to its core, one step at a time.

The Role of Leadership in Shaping Culture

David Lawson stood at the head of the conference room, looking at the faces of Innovatech's senior leadership team. The previous discussions had set the stage, but now it was time to tackle a critical aspect of their cultural transformation: leadership.

"To reignite Innovatech's culture, we must first understand the pivotal role of leadership in shaping it," David began. "Leadership isn't just about making decisions and driving strategy. It's about embodying the values and behaviors you want to see in your organization."

Sarah Mitchell, the CEO, nodded thoughtfully. She knew this session was crucial for her and her team. David gestured towards her.

"Sarah, as the CEO, your actions and attitudes set the tone for the entire company. Your employees look to you for cues on how to behave, communicate, and prioritize their work. What you do and say has a profound impact on the organizational culture."

Sarah leaned forward. "I understand that, David. But how can we ensure that our leadership aligns with the culture we want to create?"

David smiled. "That's exactly what we're here to figure out. Let's start by examining some key elements of leadership that influence culture."

He clicked the remote, and a slide appeared on the screen, listing the following points: Vision, Communication, Behavior, Recognition, Decision-Making, and Accountability.

"First, Vision," David said, pointing to the screen. "A strong leader must have a clear and compelling vision for the future.

This vision should inspire and motivate your employees. Sarah, you mentioned Innovatech's founding values yesterday. How do you see them shaping your vision for the future?"

Sarah thought for a moment. "I see Innovatech as a place where innovation thrives, where collaboration is second nature, and where every employee feels respected and included. Our vision should reflect these values and guide us towards new heights of creativity and success."

"Excellent," David replied. "Next, Communication. Effective leaders communicate their vision and values clearly and consistently. They create open channels for feedback and ensure that their message resonates throughout the organization."

Lisa, the marketing director, raised her hand. "We've struggled with communication lately. There are so many silos, and messages often get lost or misinterpreted."

David nodded. "That's a common challenge. We'll need to implement strategies to break down these silos and foster more transparent and effective communication."

He moved to the next point. "Behavior. Leaders must model the behaviors they want to see in their employees. This means demonstrating collaboration, respect, and inclusivity in every interaction."

Mark, the head of engineering, chimed in. "I've noticed that when leaders don't practice what they preach, it creates a lot of cynicism and disengagement among employees."

"Precisely," David agreed. "Authenticity is key. Your actions must align with your words. Employees need to see that you genuinely live the values you promote."

"Recognition is another crucial aspect," David continued. "Acknowledging and rewarding the right behaviors reinforces the culture you want to build. How do you currently recognize your employees' contributions?"

Tom, the HR manager, responded. "We have some recognition programs, but they're not as effective as they could be. People feel like their efforts go unnoticed."

"That's something we'll need to address," David said. "Consistent and meaningful recognition can significantly boost morale and reinforce positive cultural traits."

"Decision-Making is also vital," David went on. "How decisions are made and communicated can either build trust or erode it. Leaders should involve employees in decision-making processes whenever possible and ensure transparency."

Sarah sighed. "We've been making decisions in a top-down manner lately, especially under pressure. I see now that it's causing frustration and disengagement."

David gave her a reassuring look. "Recognizing the issue is the first step to fixing it. Finally, Accountability. Leaders must hold themselves and others accountable to the organization's values and standards. This means addressing issues promptly and fairly."

As the session wrapped up, David summarized, "Leadership is the cornerstone of organizational culture. By aligning your vision, communication, behavior, recognition, decision-making, and accountability with your core values, you can shape a culture that reflects the heart of Innovatech."

Sarah stood up, her resolve clear. "Thank you, David. We have our work cut out for us, but I believe in this team. Together, we can lead Innovatech back to its true self."

David smiled, feeling the energy and determination in the room. The leaders of Innovatech were ready to embrace their roles in shaping the company's culture, and with their commitment, the heart of Innovatech would soon beat stronger than ever.

The Impact of Culture on Business Success

David Lawson stood before the Innovatech leadership team, ready to delve into a topic that would tie together their previous discussions: the impact of culture on business success. The room was filled with anticipation, the air buzzing with a newfound sense of purpose.

"Now that we've covered the foundational elements of organizational culture, it's time to discuss why this all matters," David began. "The culture you cultivate within Innovatech directly impacts your business success. It's not just about creating a pleasant work environment; it's about driving performance, innovation, and growth."

He clicked the remote, and a new slide appeared, displaying a chart showing the correlation between strong organizational culture and business metrics such as employee retention, customer satisfaction, and profitability.

"Let's start with employee retention," David said. "A strong, positive culture reduces turnover. When employees feel valued, engaged, and aligned with the company's values, they're more likely to stay. High turnover costs time, money, and morale. How has turnover impacted Innovatech recently?"

Tom, the HR manager, grimaced. "Our turnover rate has been climbing steadily over the past two years. It's been a struggle to retain top talent, and recruiting new employees is becoming increasingly difficult."

David nodded. "That's a clear sign of cultural issues. Employees are the heart of your company. When they leave, they take valuable knowledge and experience with them, which disrupts operations and innovation."

He moved to the next point. "Now, let's talk about customer satisfaction. A positive internal culture often translates to better customer experiences. When employees are happy and engaged, they're more motivated to provide excellent service. Sarah, how has Innovatech's customer feedback been lately?"

Sarah sighed. "We've received more complaints and lower satisfaction scores. Our customers used to rave about our service and products, but that's changed."

"Customer satisfaction is a direct reflection of employee satisfaction," David explained. "Your customers can sense when your employees are disengaged or unhappy. It affects their interactions and overall experience with your brand."

David clicked to another slide showing the relationship between culture and innovation. "Innovation is another critical area. A supportive culture encourages risk-taking and creativity. It allows employees to experiment and come up with groundbreaking ideas. Mark, how has the innovation pipeline been?"

Mark, the head of engineering, looked frustrated. "Our innovation has stagnated. We used to be leaders in our field, but now we're struggling to keep up with competitors. It feels like the creative spark is gone."

"A stifled culture often leads to a stifled innovation pipeline," David said. "When employees are afraid to take risks or their ideas are not valued, innovation suffers. Reigniting that creative spark requires a culture that celebrates experimentation and learning from failure."

David then highlighted financial performance. "Profitability is also influenced by culture. Companies with strong cultures often see higher financial returns. Engaged employees are more productive, efficient, and committed to the company's success. They take fewer sick days, are more motivated, and go the extra mile."

Lisa, the marketing director, interjected. "It makes sense. When we were at our peak, our financial performance reflected it. We were all motivated and passionate about our work, and it showed in the results."

"Exactly," David said. "A thriving culture fuels a thriving business. When you invest in your culture, you invest in your bottom line."

He paused, letting the information sink in. "The impact of culture on business success is profound. It touches every aspect of your operations, from employee retention to customer satisfaction, innovation, and financial performance. By prioritizing and nurturing your organizational culture, you're setting the foundation for sustained success."

Sarah stood up, addressing her team. "We've heard the issues and seen the data. It's clear that our culture is at the core of our current challenges. But it's also clear that by focusing on our culture, we can turn things around. We have the potential to restore Innovatech to its former glory and beyond."

David smiled, feeling the energy in the room shift towards action and optimism. "You're absolutely right, Sarah. By committing to this cultural transformation, you're not just improving the workplace; you're driving the entire company towards a brighter, more successful future."

The leadership team left the room with a renewed sense of determination. They now understood the vital link between their company's culture and its success, and they were ready to take the necessary steps to rebuild the heart of Innovatech.

CHAPTER 1: UNDERSTANDING ORGANIZATIONAL CULTURE

Cultural Frameworks and Models

David Lawson reconvened with Innovatech's leadership team the following morning. The atmosphere was charged with a sense of urgency and anticipation. After discussing the impact of culture on business success, it was time to provide the team with tangible tools to rebuild their company's culture.

"Good morning, everyone," David greeted, as the team settled in. "Today, we'll explore various cultural frameworks and models that can guide us in shaping Innovatech's future. These frameworks will help us diagnose current issues and develop a clear path forward."

He clicked the remote, and a slide appeared on the screen with a colorful diagram of Edgar Schein's Organizational Culture Model.

"Let's start with Edgar Schein's model," David began. "Schein's framework breaks down organizational culture into three levels: artifacts, espoused values, and basic underlying assumptions."

He pointed to the diagram. "Artifacts are the visible elements of culture – the way your office is designed, the dress code, and the company rituals. Espoused values are the stated norms and standards, like your mission statement and code of conduct. Basic underlying assumptions are the deeply ingrained beliefs and values that are often taken for granted."

Tom, the HR manager, raised his hand. "How do we identify these basic underlying assumptions if they're not immediately visible?"

"Great question, Tom," David replied. "We can uncover these assumptions through in-depth interviews, employee surveys, and by observing everyday behaviors and decision-making patterns. Understanding these underlying assumptions will help us address the root causes of cultural issues."

David clicked to the next slide, displaying Geert Hofstede's Cultural Dimensions Theory.

"Another useful framework is Hofstede's Cultural Dimensions Theory," David continued. "Hofstede identifies six dimensions that can be used to analyze organizational culture: Power Distance, Individualism vs. Collectivism, Masculinity vs. Femininity, Uncertainty Avoidance, Long-Term vs. Short-Term Orientation, and Indulgence vs. Restraint."

He paused to let the team absorb the information. "By evaluating where Innovatech falls on these dimensions, we can gain insights into how your culture influences behavior and decision-making. For example, if there's a high power distance, it means there's a significant gap between leadership and employees, which can hinder open communication and collaboration."

Sarah Mitchell, the CEO, leaned forward. "I think Innovatech has a higher power distance than we'd like to admit. There's a noticeable divide between the executive team and the rest of the employees."

David nodded. "That's an important observation, Sarah. Reducing power distance can foster a more inclusive and communicative culture."

He moved to the next slide, which showed the Competing Values Framework by Cameron and Quinn.

"The Competing Values Framework is another powerful tool," David explained. "It categorizes organizational cultures into four types: Clan, Adhocracy, Market, and Hierarchy. Each type has its own strengths and challenges."

He pointed to each quadrant. "A Clan culture is family-like, emphasizing collaboration and employee development. An Adhocracy culture is dynamic and entrepreneurial, valuing innovation and risk-taking. A Market culture is results-oriented, focusing on competition and achieving targets. A Hierarchy culture is structured and controlled, prioritizing efficiency and stability."

Mark, the head of engineering, spoke up. "Innovatech used to be more of an Adhocracy, but we've shifted towards a Market culture. I think that's part of why we've lost some of our innovative edge."

"Interesting insight, Mark," David said. "Balancing these cultural types can be challenging, but it's crucial to find the right mix that aligns with your strategic goals and core values."

David then introduced the Denison Organizational Culture Model, displaying it on the screen.

"The Denison Model focuses on four key traits of organizational culture: Involvement, Consistency, Adaptability, and Mission," David explained. "High involvement means employees are engaged and empowered. Consistency ensures that values and systems are aligned across the organization. Adaptability allows the company to respond to changes and innovate. Mission provides a clear direction and purpose."

Lisa, the marketing director, interjected. "We've been lacking consistency. Our values aren't reflected in our daily operations, and it's causing confusion and frustration among employees."

"Consistency is indeed vital," David agreed. "We need to ensure that your values are consistently applied in every aspect of the organization, from decision-making to everyday interactions."

As David wrapped up, he summarized, "These frameworks provide us with different lenses to analyze and shape Innovatech's culture. By leveraging these models, we can diagnose current issues, identify strengths and weaknesses, and develop a cohesive cultural strategy."

Sarah stood up, addressing her team. "We've got the tools and the knowledge. Now it's time to put them into action. Let's use these frameworks to rebuild Innovatech's culture and lead our company to new heights."

David felt a sense of accomplishment as he watched the leadership team engage with the material. They were ready to embrace these frameworks and models to transform Innovatech's culture, setting the stage for a brighter, more successful future.

Assessing Your Current Culture

David Lawson knew the final step in this chapter was the most crucial. After defining culture, understanding its history, recognizing leadership's role, acknowledging its impact on business success, and exploring cultural frameworks, it was time for Innovatech to take a hard look at its current culture.

As the leadership team assembled in the conference room, David sensed their readiness to dive into the heart of the matter.

"Good morning, everyone," David began. "Today, we're going to assess Innovatech's current culture. This assessment will be our baseline, helping us understand where we are and what needs to change."

He clicked the remote, and a slide titled "Assessing Your Current Culture" appeared on the screen, featuring a multi-step process: Surveys, Interviews, Observations, and Data Analysis.

CHAPTER 1: UNDERSTANDING ORGANIZATIONAL CULTURE

"We'll start with surveys," David said. "Surveys are an effective way to gather a broad range of insights from your employees. They allow anonymity, encouraging honest feedback. We've developed a customized survey for Innovatech, which will be distributed company-wide. It covers key areas like employee engagement, communication, leadership, and values alignment."

Sarah Mitchell, the CEO, looked concerned. "How do we ensure that employees trust the process and feel safe to share their true feelings?"

"Great question, Sarah," David replied. "Transparency is key. We need to communicate the purpose of the survey clearly and assure employees that their responses will be confidential and used to improve the organization."

He moved on to the next point. "In addition to surveys, we'll conduct in-depth interviews with a representative sample of employees from various departments and levels. These interviews will provide deeper insights into specific issues and allow us to explore themes that emerge from the surveys."

Tom, the HR manager, raised his hand. "Who will conduct these interviews, and what should we focus on?"

"We'll have a mix of internal and external facilitators," David explained. "The focus will be on understanding employees' perceptions of the company's culture, their experiences, and their suggestions for improvement. We'll ask open-ended questions to encourage detailed responses."

David then highlighted the importance of observations. "Observations are another vital tool. By observing everyday interactions, meetings, and decision-making processes, we can identify cultural patterns and behaviors that surveys and interviews might miss."

Mark, the head of engineering, looked intrigued. "What specifically should we be observing?"

"We'll look at communication styles, team dynamics, leadership behaviors, and how values are reflected in daily activities," David said. "Observations provide a real-time snapshot of your culture in action."

He moved to the final point: data analysis. "We'll analyze all the data collected from surveys, interviews, and observations to identify key themes and areas for improvement. This comprehensive analysis will help us pinpoint cultural strengths and weaknesses."

Lisa, the marketing director, interjected. "What kind of themes should we expect to find?"

"Common themes might include issues related to communication, trust, leadership effectiveness, alignment with core values, and overall employee engagement," David explained. "We'll also look for inconsistencies between different departments and levels within the organization."

David clicked to a new slide titled "Engaging Employees in the Assessment Process."

"Engaging employees throughout this process is crucial," he emphasized. "We need to involve them in interpreting the data and developing action plans. This approach not only ensures buy-in but also leverages their insights and creativity."

Sarah stood up, addressing her team. "We're ready for this. Let's approach this assessment with an open mind and a commitment to listening and learning. Our employees are our greatest asset, and their voices will guide us in rebuilding our culture."

David felt a sense of momentum building. The leadership team was fully on board, ready to embark on this introspective journey.

"We'll begin the survey distribution and interview scheduling this week," David concluded. "In the meantime, I encourage each of you to start observing interactions within your teams and noting any cultural patterns you see."

As the meeting adjourned, the leaders dispersed with a renewed sense of purpose. They were about to embark on a journey of self-discovery, delving into the intricacies of Innovatech's culture to pave the way for a brighter, more cohesive future. David felt confident that this thorough assessment would provide the insights needed to rebuild the heart of Innovatech and lead it to new heights of success.

2

Chapter 2: Creating a Vision and Mission

Crafting a Clear Vision Statement

David Lawson felt a renewed energy as he walked into the Innovatech headquarters for the next session. The leadership team had taken the first steps toward understanding their culture, and now it was time to create a vision that would inspire and guide the entire company.

As the team assembled, Sarah Mitchell, the CEO, called the meeting to order. "Good morning, everyone. Today, we'll be focusing on crafting a clear vision statement for Innovatech. Our vision will serve as the North Star, guiding our actions and decisions."

David stood up, addressing the team. "A vision statement is more than just a string of words; it's a declaration of what your organization aspires to be. It should be inspiring, clear, and align with your core values."

He clicked the remote, and a slide titled "Crafting a Vision

Statement" appeared on the screen, with the following steps outlined: Reflect on Core Values, Imagine the Future, Make It Inspirational, Keep It Concise, and Ensure Alignment.

"Let's start by reflecting on your core values," David began. "Your vision should be rooted in the values that define Innovatech. What are the values that you hold most dear?"

Sarah nodded and began. "Innovation, collaboration, respect, and inclusivity. These are the pillars of Innovatech."

David smiled. "Great. Now, let's imagine the future. Where do you see Innovatech in five, ten, or even twenty years? What do you want to achieve?"

Mark, the head of engineering, spoke up. "I envision Innovatech leading the industry in technological innovation, creating products that change the world."

Lisa, the marketing director, added, "I see a company where employees are excited to come to work every day, where our culture is a magnet for top talent, and where our customer relationships are stronger than ever."

"Excellent," David said. "Your vision should be inspirational, something that excites and motivates everyone in the organization. It should capture the essence of what you want Innovatech to become."

He moved to the next point. "Keep it concise. A vision statement should be easy to remember and communicate. Aim for a few powerful sentences that convey your aspirations clearly."

Tom, the HR manager, asked, "How do we ensure that it's not just words on a paper, but something that everyone can rally behind?"

"That's where alignment comes in," David replied. "Your vision must resonate with your employees, customers, and stakeholders. It should reflect their hopes and dreams for Innovatech and be something they can see themselves contributing to."

David handed out worksheets to each team member. "I want you all to take a few minutes to draft your own vision statement for Innovatech, based on the steps we've discussed. Think about what inspires you and how you see the future of this company."

The room fell silent as the team began to write. After several minutes, David called for attention. "Let's share our drafts and see how we can combine our ideas into a cohesive vision statement."

Sarah read hers first. "Innovatech will be the global leader in innovation, fostering a culture where creativity and collaboration thrive, and making a positive impact on the world through cutting-edge technology."

Mark followed. "Innovatech will set the standard for technological advancements, creating a workplace where every employee feels valued and inspired to push the boundaries of what's possible."

Lisa added, "Innovatech will be a beacon of innovation and inclusivity, driving progress through collaboration and respect, and building lasting relationships with our customers."

David nodded, impressed by the depth and passion in their statements. "These are all fantastic visions. Now, let's work together to merge them into one powerful statement."

The team brainstormed, debated, and refined their ideas, each contributing to the evolving vision. After an intense session of collaboration, they crafted a unified vision statement:

"Innovatech will be the global leader in innovation, where creativity and collaboration thrive. We will push the boundaries of technology to make a positive impact on the world, fostering a culture of inclusivity, respect, and inspiration for all."

David smiled as he read the final statement aloud. "This is a vision that captures the essence of Innovatech. It's clear, inspirational, and aligned with your core values. This will guide you as you rebuild your culture and strive for success."

Sarah looked around the room, seeing the nods of agreement and the spark of excitement in her team's eyes. "Thank you, David. This vision is exactly what we needed. It's time to share it with the rest of Innovatech and start living it every day."

With the vision statement in hand, the leadership team felt a renewed sense of purpose. They were ready to lead Innovatech into a future filled with promise and possibility, guided by a vision that spoke to their hearts and aspirations. David felt proud of their progress, knowing that this was just the beginning of their journey towards a brighter, more unified future.

Defining Core Values and Principles

After crafting a clear vision statement for Innovatech, the leadership team gathered once again to define the core values and principles that would underpin their vision. David Lawson sensed the anticipation in the room as they prepared to delve into this crucial aspect of their cultural transformation.

"Good morning, everyone," Sarah Mitchell, the CEO, began. "Now that we have our vision in place, it's time to define the core values and principles that will guide us on our journey. These values will serve as the foundation of our culture, shaping how we behave and interact as a company."

David nodded in agreement. "Your core values are the fundamental beliefs that define who you are as an organization. They should be timeless, enduring, and non-negotiable."

He clicked the remote, and a slide titled "Defining Core Values and Principles" appeared on the screen, with the following steps outlined: Reflect on Beliefs and Behaviors, Identify Key Themes, Prioritize Values, and Articulate Principles.

"Let's start by reflecting on your beliefs and behaviors," David continued. "Think about the qualities that are most important to you as individuals and as a company. What principles do you want to uphold in everything you do?"

Tom, the HR manager, raised his hand. "How do we ensure that our core values are more than just words on a page, but something that guides our actions every day?"

"That's a great question, Tom," David replied. "To make your core values meaningful, they need to be ingrained in your company's culture and reinforced through actions, policies, and decision-making processes."

He moved to the next point. "Identify key themes. Look for common threads in your beliefs and behaviors. What recurring themes emerge from your reflections?"

Lisa, the marketing director, spoke up. "I think integrity is a key theme for us. We want to be honest and transparent in everything we do, both internally and externally."

Mark, the head of engineering, added, "Innovation is another important theme. We want to encourage creativity and experimentation, even if it means taking risks."

David nodded. "These are excellent starting points. Now, let's prioritize your values. Focus on the qualities that are essential to your vision and mission. What values will guide you in achieving your goals?"

CHAPTER 2: CREATING A VISION AND MISSION

Sarah looked around the room, considering their options. "I think collaboration is a top priority for us. We believe in the power of teamwork and cooperation to drive innovation and success."

After a thoughtful discussion, the team agreed on a set of core values: Integrity, Innovation, Collaboration, Respect, and Accountability.

"Now that we've defined our core values, let's articulate the principles that will guide our behavior and decision-making," David said. "Principles are actionable statements that embody your values in action."

He handed out worksheets to each team member. "I want you to take a few minutes to brainstorm principles that align with each of our core values. Think about specific behaviors and attitudes that reflect these values in practice."

The room buzzed with activity as the team members wrote down their ideas. After several minutes, they reconvened to share their thoughts.

Tom read aloud from his worksheet. "Under Integrity, we could have a principle like 'Always be honest and transparent in our communications and actions, even when it's difficult.'"

Lisa added, "For Innovation, how about 'Embrace change and encourage creativity, continuously seeking new ideas and solutions?'"

Mark suggested, "Under Collaboration, we could have 'Foster a culture of teamwork and open communication, valuing diverse perspectives and contributions.'"

As they worked through each core value, they articulated a set of principles that reflected their beliefs and aspirations for Innovatech.

David nodded in approval as he reviewed the list. "These

principles capture the essence of who we are and what we stand for as a company. They will guide us in our daily interactions and decision-making processes, helping us to live our core values and achieve our vision."

Sarah smiled, feeling a sense of pride in what they had accomplished. "Thank you, David. These core values and principles will be the compass that guides us on our journey. Let's make sure they're not just words on a page, but the foundation of our culture."

With their core values and principles defined, the leadership team felt a renewed sense of purpose and direction. They were ready to embrace these guiding principles and lead Innovatech towards a future filled with integrity, innovation, collaboration, respect, and accountability. David felt optimistic about the journey ahead, knowing that they were laying the groundwork for a culture that would drive their success for years to come.

Aligning Vision with Organizational Goals

As the leadership team of Innovatech gathered for their next meeting, the focus shifted to aligning their newly crafted vision with the organization's goals. David Lawson sensed the importance of this step in ensuring that their vision would drive meaningful progress and success.

"Good morning, everyone," Sarah Mitchell, the CEO, greeted. "Now that we have a clear vision statement and defined core values and principles, it's time to align our vision with our organizational goals. Our vision should serve as the guiding light for everything we do as a company."

David nodded in agreement. "Aligning your vision with your goals ensures that your aspirations translate into tangible

CHAPTER 2: CREATING A VISION AND MISSION

actions and outcomes. It's about bridging the gap between your long-term vision and your short-term objectives."

He clicked the remote, and a slide titled "Aligning Vision with Organizational Goals" appeared on the screen, with the following steps outlined: Review Current Goals, Identify Alignment, Set SMART Objectives, and Develop Action Plans.

"Let's start by reviewing our current goals," David began. "What are the key objectives that Innovatech is currently working towards?"

Tom, the HR manager, shared a list of goals from their recent strategic planning sessions. "We have goals related to product development, market expansion, employee engagement, and financial performance."

David nodded. "Now, let's identify alignment between these goals and our vision statement. How do our goals support the realization of our vision?"

Lisa, the marketing director, pointed out, "Our goal to expand into new markets aligns with our vision of becoming a global leader in innovation."

Mark, the head of engineering, added, "And our goal to increase employee engagement supports our vision of fostering a culture where creativity and collaboration thrive."

David smiled. "Exactly. By identifying alignment between our goals and our vision, we ensure that every initiative we pursue moves us closer to realizing our long-term aspirations."

He moved to the next point. "Now, let's set SMART objectives for each goal. SMART stands for Specific, Measurable, Achievable, Relevant, and Time-bound. These objectives provide clear targets and milestones to track our progress."

Sarah raised her hand. "How do we ensure that our objectives are truly aligned with our vision and not just arbitrary targets?"

"That's a great question, Sarah," David replied. "Each objective should directly contribute to the fulfillment of our vision and reflect our core values and principles. If an objective doesn't align with our vision, we need to reevaluate its importance and relevance."

The team worked together to set SMART objectives for each of their goals, ensuring that they were specific, measurable, achievable, relevant, and time-bound.

Finally, David guided them in developing action plans for each objective, outlining the steps, resources, and responsibilities required to achieve them.

"As we implement these action plans, it's important to continuously monitor our progress and make adjustments as needed," David emphasized. "Our vision should be at the forefront of every decision we make, guiding us towards a future that aligns with our aspirations and values."

Sarah stood up, feeling a renewed sense of clarity and purpose. "Thank you, David. Aligning our vision with our organizational goals has helped us see the path forward more clearly. Let's commit to living our vision every day and working towards its realization with determination and focus."

With their vision aligned with their organizational goals, the leadership team of Innovatech felt empowered and inspired. They were ready to embark on the journey towards their vision with confidence and determination, knowing that their goals were not just targets to achieve, but stepping stones towards a future filled with innovation, collaboration, and success. David felt proud of their progress and excited for the possibilities that lay ahead as they worked together to turn their vision into reality.

Communicating Vision and Mission Effectively

With their vision aligned with organizational goals, the next crucial step for the leadership team of Innovatech was to effectively communicate their vision and mission throughout the organization. David Lawson understood the importance of ensuring that every employee understood and embraced the company's aspirations.

"Good morning, everyone," Sarah Mitchell, the CEO, greeted as the team gathered for their meeting. "Now that we have a clear vision and mission, it's essential that we communicate it effectively to all our employees. Our vision should not just be words on a page but a guiding force that inspires and motivates everyone in the organization."

David nodded in agreement. "Communicating your vision and mission effectively is key to building buy-in and commitment from your employees. It's about creating a shared sense of purpose and direction."

He clicked the remote, and a slide titled "Communicating Vision and Mission Effectively" appeared on the screen, with the following steps outlined: Develop a Communication Plan, Utilize Multiple Channels, Lead by Example, and Provide Ongoing Reinforcement.

"Let's start by developing a communication plan," David began. "We need to outline how we'll share our vision and mission with all employees, ensuring that everyone understands and internalizes it."

Tom, the HR manager, suggested, "We could hold a company-wide meeting to unveil the vision and mission, followed by smaller departmental meetings to discuss how it relates to each team's work."

David nodded in agreement. "That sounds like a great approach. We also need to utilize multiple channels to reach all employees, including email, intranet, newsletters, and social media."

Lisa, the marketing director, added, "We could create visual materials like posters and infographics to reinforce the message and make it more engaging."

"Absolutely," David agreed. "Visual aids can be powerful tools for reinforcing key messages and keeping the vision and mission top of mind."

He moved to the next point. "Leading by example is also crucial. As leaders, we need to embody the values and principles outlined in our vision and mission. Our actions should align with our words, demonstrating our commitment to these ideals."

Sarah nodded. "It's important that our employees see us living our values every day. That's what will truly inspire them to do the same."

Finally, David emphasized the need for ongoing reinforcement. "Communicating our vision and mission is not a one-time event. We need to continually reinforce the message through regular updates, recognition of behaviors that align with our values, and storytelling."

Mark, the head of engineering, spoke up. "How do we ensure that our message resonates with employees at all levels of the organization?"

"We need to tailor our communication to different audiences," David replied. "Each department and level may have unique concerns and perspectives, so we need to adapt our messaging to address their specific needs and interests."

Sarah stood up, feeling a sense of excitement and determination. "Thank you, David. Effectively communicating our vision and mission is essential to rallying our employees behind a common purpose. Let's make sure that everyone in Innovatech understands and embraces our aspirations."

With their communication plan in place, the leadership team of Innovatech felt confident in their ability to share their vision and mission with the entire organization. They were ready to inspire and motivate their employees, turning their shared aspirations into reality. David felt a sense of pride in their progress and optimism for the future as they embarked on this next phase of their cultural transformation journey.

Engaging Employees in the Vision

As the leadership team of Innovatech continued their journey to embed the company's vision and mission into the fabric of their culture, they recognized the importance of actively engaging their employees in the process. David Lawson knew that true cultural transformation could only occur when every member of the organization felt a sense of ownership and commitment to the vision.

"Good morning, everyone," Sarah Mitchell, the CEO, greeted warmly as the team gathered once again. "Now that we've communicated our vision and mission, it's time to engage our employees in bringing it to life. Our success depends on their buy-in and active participation."

David nodded in agreement. "Engaging employees in the vision is crucial for building a culture where everyone feels connected to the company's purpose and motivated to contribute their best."

He clicked the remote, and a slide titled "Engaging Employees in the Vision" appeared on the screen, with the following steps outlined: Foster Open Dialogue, Encourage Feedback and Ideas, Recognize and Celebrate Contributions, and Empower Employees to Take Ownership.

"Let's start by fostering open dialogue," David began. "We need to create opportunities for employees to ask questions, share their thoughts, and express their concerns about the vision and mission."

Tom, the HR manager, suggested, "We could organize town hall meetings where employees can interact with leadership and discuss how the vision relates to their roles and responsibilities."

David nodded. "That's a great idea. It's important that employees feel heard and valued in this process."

Lisa, the marketing director, added, "We should also encourage feedback and ideas from employees on how we can further align our actions with the vision and mission."

"Absolutely," David agreed. "Employees often have valuable insights and perspectives that can help us refine our approach and make our vision more relevant and impactful."

He moved to the next point. "Recognizing and celebrating contributions is also key. When employees demonstrate behaviors that align with our values and support our vision, we should acknowledge and appreciate their efforts."

Sarah smiled. "Recognition doesn't have to be elaborate. Sometimes a simple thank you or shout-out in a team meeting can go a long way in motivating employees and reinforcing the desired behaviors."

Finally, David emphasized the need to empower employees to take ownership of the vision. "We need to provide employees with the tools, resources, and autonomy they need to contribute to the realization of our vision. When employees feel empowered to make a difference, they become more engaged and committed to the company's success."

Mark, the head of engineering, spoke up. "How do we ensure that employees understand how their individual contributions contribute to the larger vision?"

"We need to connect the dots for them," David replied. "We should clearly communicate how each employee's work directly supports the achievement of our goals and the fulfillment of our vision. When employees see the impact of their contributions, they're more motivated to excel."

Sarah stood up, feeling a sense of excitement and determination. "Thank you, David. Engaging our employees in the vision is essential for building a culture of ownership and accountability. Let's empower our employees to be champions of our vision and drive our company towards success."

With their commitment to engaging employees in the vision, the leadership team of Innovatech felt confident that they were on the right path towards building a culture where everyone felt inspired, empowered, and connected to the company's purpose. David felt a sense of pride in their progress and optimism for the future as they continued to nurture their vision and mission within the organization.

Measuring Alignment and Impact

As the leadership team of Innovatech neared the conclusion of their efforts to embed the company's vision and mission into their culture, they recognized the importance of measuring the alignment of their employees with the vision and assessing its impact on the organization. David Lawson understood that without proper measurement and evaluation, they would be unable to gauge the effectiveness of their cultural transformation efforts.

"Good morning, everyone," Sarah Mitchell, the CEO, greeted as the team assembled for their meeting. "Now that we've engaged our employees in the vision, it's crucial that we measure the alignment of our workforce with our vision and assess its impact on our organization."

David nodded in agreement. "Measuring alignment and impact allows us to evaluate the effectiveness of our cultural transformation efforts and identify areas for improvement."

He clicked the remote, and a slide titled "Measuring Alignment and Impact" appeared on the screen, with the following steps outlined: Conduct Surveys and Assessments, Analyze Data, Identify Gaps and Opportunities, and Adjust Strategies as Needed.

"Let's start by conducting surveys and assessments," David began. "We need to gather feedback from employees to understand their level of alignment with the vision and mission, as well as their perceptions of its impact on their work and the organization as a whole."

Tom, the HR manager, suggested, "We could administer a follow-up survey to assess employees' understanding of the vision, their commitment to its principles, and any obstacles they may be facing in aligning their work with the vision."

David nodded. "That's a great idea. We should also consider conducting focus groups or interviews to gather more in-depth insights from employees."

Lisa, the marketing director, added, "We should also look at key performance indicators (KPIs) related to employee engagement, productivity, and satisfaction to assess the impact of the vision on our organization."

"Absolutely," David agreed. "Analyzing data from surveys, assessments, and KPIs will help us identify areas where alignment is strong and areas where there may be gaps or opportunities for improvement."

He moved to the next point. "Once we've analyzed the data, we need to identify specific gaps and opportunities for enhancing alignment and maximizing the impact of our vision and mission."

Sarah raised her hand. "How do we ensure that our assessment is comprehensive and captures all relevant aspects of alignment and impact?"

"We need to look at both quantitative and qualitative data," David replied. "Quantitative data provides us with numerical insights, while qualitative data offers deeper insights into employees' perceptions and experiences."

Finally, David emphasized the importance of adjusting strategies based on the findings of their assessment. "We need to be willing to adapt our approach and initiatives based on the feedback we receive. This may involve refining our communication strategies, implementing targeted training programs, or making organizational changes to better support our vision and mission."

Mark, the head of engineering, spoke up. "How do we ensure that our efforts to measure alignment and impact are ongoing and not just a one-time exercise?"

"We need to build measurement and evaluation into our regular processes and routines," David replied. "This could involve conducting annual surveys, quarterly assessments, or ongoing feedback mechanisms to continually monitor alignment and impact."

Sarah stood up, feeling a sense of determination and purpose. "Thank you, David. Measuring alignment and impact is essential for ensuring that our vision and mission are not just lofty ideals, but tangible drivers of our success. Let's commit to continually assessing and refining our efforts to build a culture that truly embodies our aspirations."

With their commitment to measuring alignment and impact, the leadership team of Innovatech felt confident that they were taking the necessary steps to ensure the long-term success of their cultural transformation efforts. David felt a sense of pride in their progress and optimism for the future as they continued to nurture and strengthen their vision and mission within the organization.

Chapter 3: Leadership and Culture

The Role of Leaders in Cultural Development

In the heart of Innovatech's headquarters, the leadership team gathered for a pivotal discussion on the role of leaders in cultural development. David Lawson knew that the success of their cultural transformation journey hinged on the leadership's ability to foster and sustain a culture aligned with the company's vision and values.

"Good morning, everyone," Sarah Mitchell, the CEO, began. "As we embark on this journey to reshape our culture, it's essential that we understand the critical role that leaders play in driving cultural development."

David nodded in agreement. "Leaders set the tone for the organization. Their actions, behaviors, and decisions shape the culture and influence how employees perceive and experience it."

He clicked the remote, and a slide titled "The Role of Leaders in Cultural Development" appeared on the screen, with the following points outlined: Lead by Example, Communicate and Reinforce Values, Foster Transparency and Trust, and Empower and Develop Employees.

"Let's start by discussing how leaders can lead by example," David began. "Leaders must embody the values and principles outlined in our vision and mission. Their actions should reflect the behaviors we want to see in our employees."

Tom, the HR manager, suggested, "We could establish leadership development programs to help our leaders understand their role in shaping the culture and develop the skills and behaviors needed to lead effectively."

David nodded. "That's a great idea. Developing our leaders' capabilities is crucial for ensuring that they have the knowledge and skills to inspire and motivate their teams."

Sarah added, "Leaders also need to communicate and reinforce our values consistently. They should regularly communicate the vision and mission, and recognize and celebrate behaviors that align with our values."

Lisa, the marketing director, spoke up. "Transparency and trust are also essential. Leaders need to be open and honest in their communications, and foster an environment where employees feel comfortable sharing their ideas and concerns."

David agreed. "Empowering and developing employees is also key. Leaders should provide opportunities for growth and development, and encourage employees to take ownership of their work and contribute to the realization of our vision."

He moved to the next point. "In addition to these actions, leaders need to hold themselves and others accountable for upholding our values and driving cultural change. This may involve providing feedback, coaching, and addressing behaviors that are inconsistent with our values."

Mark, the head of engineering, spoke up. "How do we ensure that our leaders are aligned and consistent in their approach to cultural development?"

"We could establish regular leadership forums or meetings where leaders can discuss their experiences, share best practices, and align on their approach to cultural development," David suggested.

Sarah stood up, feeling a sense of determination and purpose. "Thank you, David. The role of leaders in cultural development is critical for building a culture that reflects our vision and values. Let's commit to leading by example, communicating and reinforcing our values, fostering transparency and trust, and empowering and developing our employees."

With their commitment to the role of leaders in cultural development, the leadership team of Innovatech felt confident that they were laying the foundation for a culture that would drive their success for years to come. David felt a sense of pride in their progress and optimism for the future as they continued to lead the organization towards its vision with determination and purpose.

Leading by Example: Model Behaviors

In the boardroom of Innovatech, the leadership team delved deeper into the importance of leading by example and modeling behaviors that reflect the company's values. David Lawson knew that for their cultural transformation to succeed, leaders needed to embody the values they wished to instill in their employees.

"Good morning, everyone," Sarah Mitchell, the CEO, greeted with a warm smile. "As leaders, it's imperative that we understand the power of our actions in shaping the culture of Innovatech. Leading by example is not just a suggestion; it's a necessity."

David nodded, his expression serious yet determined. "Our actions as leaders speak louder than words. Employees look to us for guidance and inspiration, and it's essential that we model the behaviors we want to see in our organization."

He clicked the remote, and a slide titled "Leading by Example: Model Behaviors" appeared on the screen, outlining key points: Consistency, Integrity, Accountability, and Empathy.

"Let's start with consistency," David began. "Consistency in our actions reinforces our commitment to our values. We must ensure that our behavior aligns with our words and that we consistently uphold the standards we expect from others."

Tom, the HR manager, raised his hand. "How do we ensure consistency across the leadership team?"

"We can establish clear expectations and guidelines for behavior," David suggested. "This could include creating a code of conduct or leadership principles that outline the expected behaviors and provide guidance on how to uphold them."

Sarah nodded in agreement. "Integrity is also paramount. We must act with honesty, transparency, and ethical conduct in all our interactions. Our integrity sets the tone for the entire organization and builds trust among employees."

Lisa, the marketing director, added, "Accountability is equally important. Leaders must take responsibility for their actions and decisions, and hold themselves and others accountable for upholding our values and achieving our goals."

David smiled at her contribution. "Exactly, Lisa. When leaders demonstrate accountability, it creates a culture of ownership and responsibility throughout the organization."

He moved on to the final point. "Finally, empathy plays a crucial role in leadership. Leaders must show empathy and understanding towards their employees, acknowledging their perspectives and emotions, and supporting them through challenges."

Mark, the head of engineering, spoke up. "How do we ensure that our actions as leaders are perceived as genuine and not just for show?"

"We need to lead with authenticity," David replied. "Our actions must stem from a genuine belief in our values and a sincere desire to create a positive and inclusive culture. When our employees see that our actions align with our words and values, they'll be more likely to trust and respect us as leaders."

Sarah stood up, feeling a sense of determination and purpose. "Thank you, David. Leading by example is not just a responsibility; it's a privilege. Let's commit to modeling the behaviors we want to see in our organization and inspiring our employees to do the same."

With their commitment to leading by example and modeling behaviors that reflect the company's values, the leadership team of Innovatech felt empowered to drive their cultural transformation forward with confidence and purpose. David felt a sense of pride in their dedication and optimism for the future as they continued to lead by example and inspire their employees to greatness.

Building Trust and Transparency

In the executive conference room of Innovatech, the leadership team gathered to discuss the critical importance of building trust and transparency within the organization. David Lawson knew that without a foundation of trust and transparency, their cultural transformation efforts would struggle to gain traction.

"Good morning, everyone," Sarah Mitchell, the CEO, greeted, her tone serious yet warm. "Trust and transparency are the cornerstones of any successful organization. As leaders, it's our responsibility to foster an environment where trust thrives and transparency reigns."

David nodded in agreement, his expression reflecting the gravity of the topic. "Trust is the bedrock of strong relationships, both within the organization and with our stakeholders. Without trust, collaboration, innovation, and growth become significantly more challenging."

He clicked the remote, and a slide titled "Building Trust and Transparency" appeared on the screen, outlining key points: Open Communication, Accountability, Honesty, and Consistency.

"Let's start with open communication," David began. "Transparent communication builds trust by keeping employees informed about the company's goals, challenges, and decisions. It's essential that we create channels for honest and open dialogue, where employees feel comfortable sharing their ideas, concerns, and feedback."

Tom, the HR manager, raised his hand. "How do we ensure that communication remains open and transparent, especially during times of change or uncertainty?"

"We can establish regular town hall meetings, Q&A sessions, and feedback channels to facilitate communication between leaders and employees," David suggested. "Leaders should also lead by example by communicating openly and honestly, even when the message may be difficult to deliver."

Sarah nodded in agreement. "Accountability is also crucial.

CHAPTER 3: LEADERSHIP AND CULTURE

Leaders must hold themselves and others accountable for their actions, decisions, and commitments. When employees see that accountability is enforced consistently, trust in leadership grows."

Lisa, the marketing director, added, "Honesty goes hand in hand with accountability. We must be truthful and upfront in our communications, even when the truth may be uncomfortable or inconvenient."

David smiled at her contribution. "Exactly, Lisa. Honesty builds credibility and strengthens trust. It's essential that we communicate with integrity and authenticity, always."

He moved on to the final point. "Consistency is also key. Leaders must be consistent in their words and actions, demonstrating reliability and predictability. When employees know what to expect from their leaders, they feel more confident and secure in their roles."

Mark, the head of engineering, spoke up. "How do we rebuild trust if it's been eroded due to past experiences or organizational changes?"

"We need to acknowledge the past, learn from it, and commit to doing better in the future," David replied. "This may involve apologizing for past mistakes, actively listening to employees' concerns, and taking concrete actions to rebuild trust over time."

Sarah stood up, feeling a sense of determination and purpose. "Thank you, David. Building trust and transparency is not just a goal; it's a journey. Let's commit to fostering an environment where trust thrives, and transparency reigns, empowering our employees to do their best work."

With their commitment to building trust and transparency, the leadership team of Innovatech felt empowered to lead their organization towards a brighter and more collaborative future. David felt a sense of optimism for the journey ahead as they continued to prioritize trust and transparency in their leadership approach.

Leadership Styles and Their Impact on Culture

In the boardroom of Innovatech, the leadership team gathered once again, this time to explore the different leadership styles and their profound impact on organizational culture. David Lawson knew that understanding the various leadership approaches was essential for shaping a culture that fostered innovation, collaboration, and growth.

"Good morning, everyone," Sarah Mitchell, the CEO, greeted, her voice carrying a note of anticipation. "As leaders, our styles and approaches have a significant influence on the culture of Innovatech. It's essential that we recognize the strengths and limitations of different leadership styles and their impact on our organization."

David nodded in agreement, his expression focused and attentive. "Leadership styles set the tone for how decisions are made, how employees are motivated, and how conflicts are resolved. By understanding the various styles, we can better align our leadership approach with the goals and values of our organization."

He clicked the remote, and a slide titled "Leadership Styles and Their Impact on Culture" appeared on the screen, outlining key points: Autocratic, Democratic, Transformational, and Servant Leadership.

"Let's start with autocratic leadership," David began. "In this style, leaders make decisions without consulting their team members, often relying on their authority and expertise. While this approach can be effective in certain situations, it can also stifle innovation and collaboration, leading to a culture of fear and resentment."

Tom, the HR manager, raised his hand. "How do we ensure that our leadership style is not overly autocratic, especially in times of crisis or urgency?"

"We can balance the need for decisive action with the importance of involving employees in the decision-making process," David suggested. "Even in times of crisis, leaders can seek input from their team members, empowering them to contribute their ideas and perspectives."

Sarah nodded in agreement. "Democratic leadership, on the other hand, involves collaborating with team members to make decisions and solve problems. This approach fosters a culture of inclusion and empowerment, where employees feel valued and engaged in the decision-making process."

Lisa, the marketing director, added, "Transformational leadership inspires and motivates employees to achieve their full potential. Leaders in this style focus on vision and values, and they empower their team members to innovate and take risks."

David smiled at her contribution. "Exactly, Lisa. Transformational leaders create a culture of creativity and excellence, where employees are encouraged to challenge the status quo and pursue ambitious goals."

He moved on to the final point. "Servant leadership revolves around serving the needs of others and putting their interests first. Leaders in this style prioritize the well-being and development of their team members, fostering a culture of empathy, collaboration, and trust."

Mark, the head of engineering, spoke up. "How do we

determine which leadership style is most appropriate for our organization?"

"We can assess the needs and goals of our organization, as well as the preferences and capabilities of our team members," David replied. "It's also important to remain flexible and adaptable, adjusting our leadership style as needed to meet the evolving needs of our organization."

Sarah stood up, feeling a sense of determination and purpose. "Thank you, David. Understanding the impact of our leadership styles on culture is essential for creating a work environment where employees thrive and succeed. Let's commit to leading with intention and empathy, inspiring our team members to reach their full potential."

With their commitment to understanding and adapting their leadership styles to the needs of their organization, the leadership team of Innovatech felt empowered to cultivate a culture of innovation, collaboration, and growth. David felt a renewed sense of purpose and optimism for the journey ahead as they continued to lead with intention and empathy, driving their organization towards success.

Developing Leadership Skills and Competencies

In the bustling meeting room of Innovatech, the leadership team convened once again, this time to explore the vital topic of developing leadership skills and competencies. David Lawson understood that investing in the development of their leaders was crucial for nurturing a culture of continuous growth and excellence.

"Good morning, everyone," Sarah Mitchell, the CEO, greeted, her tone filled with energy and enthusiasm. "As leaders, it's imperative that we continually strive to develop our skills and competencies. Our ability to lead effectively directly impacts the culture and success of Innovatech."

David nodded in agreement, his expression reflecting a deep commitment to personal and professional growth. "Leadership development is not just about acquiring new skills; it's about becoming better versions of ourselves and inspiring others to do the same."

He clicked the remote, and a slide titled "Developing Leadership Skills and Competencies" appeared on the screen, outlining key points: Self-awareness, Communication, Emotional Intelligence, Decision-making, and Adaptability.

"Let's start with self-awareness," David began. "Self-aware leaders understand their strengths, weaknesses, and areas for growth. By knowing ourselves deeply, we can better understand how our behaviors and decisions impact others and the organization as a whole."

Tom, the HR manager, raised his hand. "How do we cultivate self-awareness among our leaders?"

"We can encourage self-reflection, feedback, and coaching," David suggested. "Leadership assessments, personality inventories, and 360-degree feedback can also provide valuable insights into our leadership style and impact."

Sarah nodded in agreement. "Communication is also a fundamental leadership skill. Effective communication fosters understanding, collaboration, and trust. As leaders, we must communicate clearly, actively listen to others, and adapt our communication style to different audiences and situations."

Lisa, the marketing director, added, "Emotional intelligence is equally important. Leaders with high emotional intelligence can navigate complex interpersonal dynamics, manage conflict effectively, and inspire and motivate their team members."

David smiled at her contribution. "Exactly, Lisa. Emotional intelligence allows us to connect with others on a deeper level and create an environment where everyone feels valued and supported."

He moved on to the next point. "Decision-making is a critical leadership competency. Leaders must make timely and well-informed decisions, weighing risks and benefits, and considering the impact on stakeholders and the organization's goals."

Mark, the head of engineering, spoke up. "How do we develop our decision-making skills?"

"We can practice decision-making through scenario-based simulations, case studies, and real-world challenges," David replied. "We can also seek input from mentors, coaches, and peers to gain different perspectives and insights."

Finally, David emphasized the importance of adaptability. "In today's rapidly changing world, leaders must be flexible and adaptable, able to pivot quickly in response to new opportunities and challenges."

Sarah stood up, feeling a sense of determination and purpose. "Thank you, David. Developing our leadership skills and competencies is not just a personal journey; it's a collective commitment to the success and growth of Innovatech. Let's embrace this opportunity for growth and continue to inspire greatness in ourselves and others."

With their commitment to developing their leadership skills and competencies, the leadership team of Innovatech felt empowered to lead their organization towards a brighter and more prosperous future. David felt a renewed sense of excitement and optimism for the journey ahead as they continued to invest in their personal and professional growth, driving their organization towards success.

Succession Planning and Leadership Continuity

In the serene atmosphere of the conference room at Innovatech, the leadership team gathered once more, this time to delve into the critical topic of succession planning and ensuring leadership continuity. David Lawson knew that preparing future leaders was essential for maintaining organizational stability and driving sustained success.

"Good morning, everyone," Sarah Mitchell, the CEO, greeted, her tone carrying a sense of purpose and foresight. "As leaders, it's our responsibility to ensure that Innovatech continues to thrive long into the future. Succession planning is key to preserving our legacy and maintaining continuity in leadership."

David nodded in agreement, his expression reflecting a sense of determination and resolve. "Succession planning involves identifying and developing future leaders who can step into key roles when needed. It's about building a pipeline of talent and ensuring that the organization is prepared for any leadership transitions."

He clicked the remote, and a slide titled "Succession Planning and Leadership Continuity" appeared on the screen, outlining key points: Identify High-Potential Talent, Provide Development Opportunities, Foster Mentorship and Coaching, and Create a Culture of Continuous Learning.

"Let's start by identifying high-potential talent within the organization," David began. "These are individuals who demonstrate the skills, capabilities, and potential to assume leadership roles in the future. By identifying and nurturing these talents early on, we can ensure a smooth transition when leadership vacancies arise."

Tom, the HR manager, raised his hand. "How do we identify high-potential talent?"

"We can use performance evaluations, talent assessments, and feedback from managers and peers to identify individuals with leadership potential," David suggested. "We can also provide opportunities for employees to self-nominate or express their interest in leadership roles."

Sarah nodded in agreement. "Once high-potential talent has been identified, it's essential to provide them with development opportunities to help them grow and prepare for future leadership roles."

Lisa, the marketing director, added, "Mentorship and coaching are powerful tools for leadership development. Experienced leaders can provide guidance, support, and feedback to emerging leaders, helping them navigate their career paths and develop the skills they need to succeed."

David smiled at her contribution. "Exactly, Lisa. Mentorship and coaching create a culture of learning and growth, where knowledge and wisdom are passed down from one generation of leaders to the next."

He moved on to the next point. "Creating a culture of continuous learning is also crucial. Leaders must be lifelong learners, committed to developing their skills and staying abreast of industry trends and best practices."

Mark, the head of engineering, spoke up. "How do we ensure that our succession planning efforts are aligned with the long-term goals and strategic priorities of the organization?"

"We can regularly review and update our succession plans to ensure that they remain aligned with the evolving needs of the organization," David replied. "This may involve revisiting our talent identification criteria, adjusting our development programs, and realigning our succession priorities as needed."

Sarah stood up, feeling a sense of determination and purpose. "Thank you, David. Succession planning is not just about preparing for leadership transitions; it's about building a strong and resilient organization that can thrive in any circumstance. Let's commit to nurturing the next generation of leaders and ensuring that Innovatech continues to lead and innovate for years to come."

With their commitment to succession planning and leadership continuity, the leadership team of Innovatech felt empowered to build a legacy of excellence and drive their organization towards sustained success. David felt a renewed sense of purpose and optimism for the journey ahead as they continued to invest in the future of their organization and its leadership.

4

Chapter 4: Employee Engagement and Motivation

Understanding Employee Engagement

In the vibrant offices of Innovatech, the leadership team gathered to delve into the crucial topic of employee engagement and motivation. David Lawson knew that understanding what drives employees to perform at their best was essential for creating a culture of productivity, innovation, and success.

"Good morning, everyone," Sarah Mitchell, the CEO, greeted, her voice resonating with warmth and enthusiasm. "As leaders, it's imperative that we understand the factors that influence employee engagement and motivation. Our ability to engage and inspire our employees directly impacts the success and growth of Innovatech."

David nodded in agreement, his expression reflecting a keen interest in exploring the intricacies of employee engagement. "Employee engagement goes beyond satisfaction or happiness at work. It's about the emotional connection employees have with their work, their colleagues, and the organization as a whole."

He clicked the remote, and a slide titled "Understanding Employee Engagement" appeared on the screen, outlining key points: Definition of Employee Engagement, Factors Influencing Employee Engagement, Benefits of Employee Engagement, and Strategies for Increasing Employee Engagement.

"Let's start by defining employee engagement," David began. "Employee engagement refers to the level of enthusiasm, commitment, and dedication employees have towards their work and the organization. Engaged employees are passionate about their roles, aligned with the company's goals, and willing to go above and beyond to contribute to its success."

Tom, the HR manager, raised his hand. "What factors influence employee engagement?"

"We can break down the factors into three main categories: organizational factors, job-related factors, and individual factors," David explained. "Organizational factors include the company's culture, leadership, and opportunities for growth and development. Job-related factors include the nature of the work, autonomy, and recognition. Individual factors include personal values, interests, and motivations."

Sarah nodded in agreement. "The benefits of employee engagement are significant. Engaged employees are more productive, innovative, and committed to the organization. They're also more likely to stay with the company, reducing turnover and recruitment costs."

Lisa, the marketing director, added, "Engaged employees also contribute to a positive work environment, fostering collaboration, creativity, and a sense of belonging."

David smiled at her contribution. "Exactly, Lisa. Employee engagement has a ripple effect, impacting not only individual performance but also team dynamics and organizational culture."

He moved on to the next point. "To increase employee engagement, we need to implement strategies that address the key drivers of engagement. This may involve creating opportunities for career advancement, providing regular feedback and recognition, fostering a culture of trust and transparency, and promoting work-life balance."

Mark, the head of engineering, spoke up. "How do we measure employee engagement?"

"We can use surveys, focus groups, and interviews to gather feedback from employees about their level of engagement," David replied. "We can also track metrics such as employee turnover, absenteeism, and productivity to gauge the overall health of employee engagement within the organization."

Sarah stood up, feeling a sense of determination and purpose. "Thank you, David. Understanding employee engagement is the first step towards creating a work environment where employees thrive and succeed. Let's commit to implementing strategies that foster engagement and motivation, empowering our employees to reach their full potential."

With their commitment to understanding and improving employee engagement, the leadership team of Innovatech felt empowered to create a culture of high performance and success. David felt a renewed sense of purpose and optimism for the journey ahead as they continued to prioritize employee engagement and motivation in their leadership approach.

Strategies for Increasing Engagement

In the dynamic atmosphere of Innovatech's meeting room, the leadership team reconvened to explore practical strategies for boosting employee engagement. David Lawson understood that implementing effective engagement strategies was crucial for fostering a culture of commitment, satisfaction, and productivity among employees.

"Good morning, everyone," Sarah Mitchell, the CEO, greeted, her tone brimming with energy and determination. "As we delve deeper into employee engagement, let's explore actionable strategies that can help us elevate engagement levels and inspire our team members to perform at their best."

David nodded in agreement, his gaze focused on the task at hand. "Increasing employee engagement requires a multifaceted approach that addresses the various factors influencing engagement. By implementing targeted strategies, we can create an environment where employees feel valued, motivated, and empowered to contribute to the organization's success."

He clicked the remote, and a slide titled "Strategies for Increasing Engagement" appeared on the screen, outlining key points: Clear Communication, Recognition and Appreciation, Opportunities for Growth and Development, Work-Life Balance, and Employee Well-being Initiatives.

"Let's start with clear communication," David began. "Transparent communication builds trust and fosters a sense of belonging among employees. Leaders should communicate openly about the company's goals, strategies, and challenges, and provide regular updates on key initiatives and decisions."

Tom, the HR manager, raised his hand. "How do we ensure that communication is effective and reaches all employees?"

"We can leverage various communication channels, such as town hall meetings, team huddles, newsletters, and digital platforms, to ensure that information is accessible and inclusive," David suggested. "Leaders should also encourage two-way communication, actively seeking input and feedback from employees and responding promptly to their questions and concerns."

Sarah nodded in agreement. "Recognition and appreciation are also powerful drivers of engagement. Employees want to feel valued and appreciated for their contributions. Recognizing their achievements, both big and small, reinforces their sense of purpose and motivates them to continue performing at their best."

Lisa, the marketing director, added, "Opportunities for growth and development are essential for engaging and retaining top talent. Employees want to know that their career progression is supported and that they have access to learning and development opportunities that align with their goals and aspirations."

David smiled at her contribution. "Exactly, Lisa. By investing in employee development, we not only enhance their skills and capabilities but also demonstrate our commitment to their long-term success and well-being."

He moved on to the next point. "Work-life balance is another critical factor in employee engagement. Employees need time to recharge and disconnect from work to avoid burnout and maintain overall well-being."

Mark, the head of engineering, spoke up. "How do we promote work-life balance in a fast-paced and demanding work environment?"

"We can encourage flexible work arrangements, such as

remote work options, flexible hours, and compressed workweeks, to accommodate employees' personal needs and preferences," David replied. "We can also establish clear boundaries around work hours and encourage employees to take regular breaks and vacations to recharge."

Sarah stood up, feeling a sense of determination and purpose. "Thank you, David. Implementing strategies for increasing engagement requires a concerted effort from all of us. Let's commit to fostering a culture where communication is clear, recognition is abundant, opportunities for growth are plentiful, work-life balance is respected, and employee well-being is prioritized."

With their commitment to implementing strategies for increasing engagement, the leadership team of Innovatech felt empowered to create a workplace where employees felt valued, motivated, and inspired to achieve greatness. David felt a renewed sense of optimism and purpose for the journey ahead as they continued to prioritize employee engagement and motivation in their leadership approach.

Recognizing and Rewarding Contributions

In the vibrant conference room of Innovatech, the leadership team delved into the importance of recognizing and rewarding employee contributions as a key strategy for boosting engagement and motivation. David Lawson knew that acknowledging and celebrating achievements played a pivotal role in fostering a culture of appreciation and excellence.

"Good morning, everyone," Sarah Mitchell, the CEO, greeted, her voice filled with warmth and enthusiasm. "Today, we're diving into the vital topic of recognizing and rewarding employee contributions. It's essential that we show appreciation for the hard work and dedication of our team members to inspire continued excellence."

David nodded in agreement, his expression reflecting a deep understanding of the significance of recognition in motivating employees. "Recognizing and rewarding contributions not only boosts morale and motivation but also reinforces desired behaviors and strengthens the bond between employees and the organization."

He clicked the remote, and a slide titled "Recognizing and Rewarding Contributions" appeared on the screen, outlining key points: Types of Recognition, Benefits of Recognition, and Strategies for Effective Recognition.

"Let's start by exploring the different types of recognition," David began. "Recognition can take many forms, including verbal praise, written commendations, public acknowledgment in meetings or newsletters, awards and certificates, and even monetary rewards or bonuses."

Tom, the HR manager, raised his hand. "How do we ensure that our recognition efforts are meaningful and impactful?"

"We can tailor our recognition efforts to align with the preferences and preferences of individual employees," David suggested. "Some employees may prefer public recognition, while others may prefer more private forms of acknowledgment. It's essential to understand what motivates each employee and customize our approach accordingly."

Sarah nodded in agreement. "The benefits of recognition extend beyond boosting morale. Recognized employees are more engaged, committed, and loyal to the organization. They also tend to be more productive and innovative, driving overall performance and success."

Lisa, the marketing director, added, "Effective recognition is timely, specific, and genuine. It's important to acknowledge contributions promptly and specifically, highlighting the impact of the employee's actions on the team or organization."

David smiled at her contribution. "Exactly, Lisa. By providing specific feedback and highlighting the value of the employee's contributions, we reinforce desired behaviors and motivate them to continue performing at their best."

He moved on to the next point. "To ensure that our recognition efforts are effective, we need to establish a culture of recognition within the organization. Leaders should lead by example, consistently recognizing and celebrating achievements, and encouraging their teams to do the same."

Mark, the head of engineering, spoke up. "How do we ensure that recognition is fair and equitable across the organization?"

"We can establish clear criteria and guidelines for recognition, ensuring that it is based on merit and aligned with the organization's values and goals," David replied. "We can also involve employees in the recognition process, soliciting nominations and feedback from peers and team members to ensure that contributions are acknowledged and valued."

Sarah stood up, feeling a sense of determination and purpose. "Thank you, David. Recognizing and rewarding contributions is not just a nice-to-have; it's a critical driver of engagement and motivation. Let's commit to creating a culture where appreciation is abundant, and every employee feels valued and recognized for their contributions."

With their commitment to recognizing and rewarding contributions, the leadership team of Innovatech felt empowered to cultivate a culture of appreciation, excellence, and success. David felt a renewed sense of optimism and purpose for the journey ahead as they continued to prioritize employee recognition and motivation in their leadership approach.

Creating a Supportive Work Environment

In the welcoming ambiance of Innovatech's meeting room, the leadership team reconvened to explore the pivotal role of creating a supportive work environment in fostering employee engagement and motivation. David Lawson understood that cultivating an atmosphere of trust, respect, and camaraderie was essential for nurturing a culture where employees could thrive and excel.

"Good morning, everyone," Sarah Mitchell, the CEO, greeted, her tone imbued with warmth and empathy. "Today, we're diving into the crucial topic of creating a supportive work environment. It's imperative that we foster a culture where employees feel valued, respected, and empowered to bring their best selves to work each day."

David nodded in agreement, his demeanor reflecting a deep commitment to fostering a positive work environment. "A supportive work environment provides employees with the resources, tools, and encouragement they need to succeed. It's a place where collaboration, innovation, and well-being are prioritized."

He clicked the remote, and a slide titled "Creating a Supportive Work Environment" appeared on the screen, outlining key points: Trust and Transparency, Collaboration and Teamwork, Work-Life Balance, and Psychological Safety.

"Let's start with trust and transparency," David began. "Trust is the foundation of any successful relationship, including the relationship between employees and the organization. Leaders

CHAPTER 4: EMPLOYEE ENGAGEMENT AND MOTIVATION

should communicate openly and honestly, involve employees in decision-making, and demonstrate integrity and consistency in their actions."

Tom, the HR manager, raised his hand. "How do we cultivate trust and transparency within the organization?"

"We can establish clear communication channels, such as regular town hall meetings, team huddles, and feedback sessions, where employees feel comfortable sharing their ideas, concerns, and feedback," David suggested. "Leaders should also lead by example, demonstrating transparency in their decision-making and actively seeking input from employees."

Sarah nodded in agreement. "Collaboration and teamwork are also essential components of a supportive work environment. When employees feel valued and respected by their colleagues, they're more likely to collaborate effectively, share knowledge and ideas, and support each other's success."

Lisa, the marketing director, added, "Promoting work-life balance is equally important. Employees need time to recharge and disconnect from work to avoid burnout and maintain overall well-being."

David smiled at her contribution. "Exactly, Lisa. By offering flexible work arrangements, promoting time off, and providing resources for stress management and work-life balance, we can create an environment where employees feel supported in managing their personal and professional responsibilities."

He moved on to the next point. "Psychological safety is another critical aspect of a supportive work environment. Employees should feel comfortable taking risks, expressing their opinions, and admitting mistakes without fear of judgment or reprisal."

Mark, the head of engineering, spoke up. "How do we

promote psychological safety within our teams?"

"We can encourage open communication, active listening, and constructive feedback," David replied. "Leaders should create an environment where diverse perspectives are valued and where employees feel empowered to speak up and contribute to discussions without fear of criticism or backlash."

Sarah stood up, feeling a sense of determination and purpose. "Thank you, David. Creating a supportive work environment is not just about policies and procedures; it's about fostering a culture where employees feel valued, respected, and empowered to succeed. Let's commit to cultivating an environment where trust, collaboration, work-life balance, and psychological safety thrive."

With their commitment to creating a supportive work environment, the leadership team of Innovatech felt empowered to nurture a culture of excellence, collaboration, and well-being. David felt a renewed sense of optimism and purpose for the journey ahead as they continued to prioritize employee engagement and motivation in their leadership approach.

Encouraging Innovation and Creativity

In the dynamic environment of Innovatech's meeting room, the leadership team reconvened to explore the critical role of encouraging innovation and creativity in fostering employee engagement and motivation. David Lawson understood that fostering a culture of innovation and creativity was essential for driving continuous improvement and staying ahead in a rapidly evolving market.

"Good morning, everyone," Sarah Mitchell, the CEO, greeted, her voice filled with energy and excitement. "Today, we're diving into the exciting topic of encouraging innovation and creativity. It's imperative that we create a culture where employees feel empowered to think outside the box, take calculated risks, and explore new ideas."

David nodded in agreement, his demeanor reflecting a deep appreciation for the importance of innovation in driving organizational success. "Encouraging innovation and creativity not only drives business growth but also engages and motivates employees by providing them with opportunities for exploration, learning, and growth."

He clicked the remote, and a slide titled "Encouraging Innovation and Creativity" appeared on the screen, outlining key points: Fostering a Culture of Curiosity, Providing Resources and Support, Celebrating Experimentation and Learning, and Recognizing and Rewarding Innovation.

"Let's start by fostering a culture of curiosity," David began. "Curiosity is the fuel for innovation. When employees are curious and inquisitive, they're more likely to explore new ideas, challenge the status quo, and seek out opportunities for improvement."

Tom, the HR manager, raised his hand. "How do we cultivate curiosity within our teams?"

"We can encourage employees to ask questions, explore new perspectives, and challenge assumptions," David suggested. "Leaders should create an environment where curiosity is valued and rewarded, and where employees feel encouraged to pursue their interests and passions."

Sarah nodded in agreement. "Providing resources and support is also crucial for fostering innovation and creativity. Employees need access to tools, training, and expertise to turn their ideas into reality."

Lisa, the marketing director, added, "Celebrating experimentation and learning is equally important. Not every idea will succeed, but every experiment is an opportunity to learn and grow. By celebrating both successes and failures, we create a culture where innovation flourishes."

David smiled at her contribution. "Exactly, Lisa. By embracing a mindset of experimentation and learning, we create an environment where employees feel empowered to take risks, try new things, and push the boundaries of what's possible."

He moved on to the next point. "Recognizing and rewarding innovation is essential for sustaining a culture of creativity. Employees should feel valued and appreciated for their contributions to innovation, whether it's through new products, processes, or ideas."

Mark, the head of engineering, spoke up. "How do we recognize and reward innovation effectively?"

"We can establish innovation awards, recognition programs, and incentives to celebrate and reward employees who contribute to innovation," David replied. "We can also provide opportunities for employees to showcase their work and share their ideas with the broader organization."

Sarah stood up, feeling a sense of determination and purpose. "Thank you, David. Encouraging innovation and creativity is not just about generating new ideas; it's about fostering a culture where every employee feels empowered to contribute to the organization's success. Let's commit to creating an environment where curiosity, experimentation, and innovation thrive."

With their commitment to encouraging innovation and creativity, the leadership team of Innovatech felt empowered to drive continuous improvement and innovation within their organization. David felt a renewed sense of optimism and purpose for the journey ahead as they continued to prioritize employee engagement and motivation in their leadership approach.

Measuring and Monitoring Engagement

In the focused atmosphere of Innovatech's meeting room, the leadership team delved into the importance of measuring and monitoring employee engagement as a crucial aspect of fostering a motivated and high-performing workforce. David Lawson understood that gathering feedback and insights about employee engagement was essential for identifying areas of improvement and driving positive change.

"Good morning, everyone," Sarah Mitchell, the CEO, greeted, her tone carrying a sense of purpose and determination. "Today, we're exploring the critical topic of measuring and monitoring employee engagement. It's imperative that we understand how our employees are feeling and what drives their commitment to the organization."

David nodded in agreement, his expression reflecting a keen interest in leveraging data to inform decision-making and enhance employee engagement. "Measuring and monitoring engagement allows us to identify trends, track progress, and implement targeted interventions to improve employee satisfaction and performance."

He clicked the remote, and a slide titled "Measuring and Monitoring Engagement" appeared on the screen, outlining key points: Employee Engagement Surveys, Pulse Surveys, Focus Groups, and Key Performance Indicators.

"Let's start with employee engagement surveys," David

began. "Engagement surveys are a valuable tool for gathering feedback from employees about their level of engagement, satisfaction, and commitment to the organization. These surveys typically include questions about job satisfaction, leadership effectiveness, communication, and opportunities for growth and development."

Tom, the HR manager, raised his hand. "How do we ensure that our engagement surveys are effective and actionable?"

"We can design surveys that are clear, concise, and focused on actionable insights," David suggested. "It's essential to ask specific questions that provide meaningful data about the factors influencing engagement and satisfaction. We can also ensure anonymity and confidentiality to encourage honest and candid feedback from employees."

Sarah nodded in agreement. "Pulse surveys are another useful tool for measuring engagement. These shorter, more frequent surveys allow us to track changes in engagement over time and respond quickly to emerging issues or trends."

Lisa, the marketing director, added, "Focus groups can provide valuable qualitative insights into employee perceptions, experiences, and needs. By bringing together small groups of employees for open discussions, we can gather rich, in-depth feedback about specific topics or areas of concern."

David smiled at her contribution. "Exactly, Lisa. Focus groups allow us to explore complex issues in more detail and gain a deeper understanding of employee perspectives and experiences."

He moved on to the next point. "Key performance indicators (KPIs) are also valuable for monitoring engagement at both the individual and organizational levels. KPIs may include metrics such as employee turnover rates, absenteeism, productivity, and customer satisfaction scores."

Mark, the head of engineering, spoke up. "How do we use KPIs to drive improvement in engagement?"

"We can establish benchmarks and targets for each KPI and track progress over time," David replied. "By monitoring KPIs regularly and comparing them against industry standards or internal benchmarks, we can identify areas for improvement and implement targeted interventions to enhance engagement and performance."

Sarah stood up, feeling a sense of determination and purpose. "Thank you, David. Measuring and monitoring engagement is not just about collecting data; it's about using insights to drive positive change and create a workplace where employees feel valued, motivated, and empowered to succeed. Let's commit to leveraging data to inform our decisions and continuously improve employee engagement."

With their commitment to measuring and monitoring engagement, the leadership team of Innovatech felt empowered to drive positive change and enhance employee satisfaction and performance. David felt a renewed sense of optimism and purpose for the journey ahead as they continued to prioritize employee engagement and motivation in their leadership approach.

Chapter 5: Communication in Organizational Culture

Effective Internal Communication Strategies

In the bustling headquarters of Innovatech, the leadership team assembled to explore the pivotal role of communication in shaping organizational culture. David Lawson understood that effective internal communication was the cornerstone of a cohesive and engaged workforce.

"Good morning, everyone," Sarah Mitchell, the CEO, greeted, her voice carrying authority and warmth. "Today, we're diving into the crucial topic of communication in organizational culture. Effective communication is essential for fostering transparency, collaboration, and alignment within the organization."

David nodded in agreement, his demeanor reflecting a deep appreciation for the power of communication in driving organizational success. "Internal communication serves as the lifeblood of our organization, connecting employees, departments, and leadership to share information, align goals, and drive engagement."

He clicked the remote, and a slide titled "Effective Internal Communication Strategies" appeared on the screen, outlining key points: Clear and Consistent Messaging, Two-Way Communication Channels, Utilizing Technology, and Engaging Visuals.

"Let's start with clear and consistent messaging," David began. "Clear communication ensures that information is conveyed accurately and effectively, reducing misunderstandings and fostering a shared understanding of organizational goals and priorities."

Tom, the HR manager, raised his hand. "How do we ensure that our messaging is clear and consistent across the organization?"

"We can establish communication protocols and guidelines to ensure consistency in messaging," David suggested. "Leaders should communicate openly and transparently, providing context and rationale behind decisions and initiatives. Consistency in messaging builds trust and credibility with employees."

Sarah nodded in agreement. "Two-way communication channels are also essential for engaging employees and soliciting feedback. Employees should feel empowered to voice their opinions, ask questions, and share ideas with leadership."

Lisa, the marketing director, added, "Utilizing technology can enhance communication efficiency and accessibility. Tools such as intranet platforms, instant messaging apps, and video conferencing enable real-time communication and collaboration, especially in a remote or distributed workforce."

David smiled at her contribution. "Exactly, Lisa. Technology allows us to bridge geographical barriers and connect employees across different locations, fostering a sense of unity and cohesion."

He moved on to the next point. "Engaging visuals can also enhance communication effectiveness by capturing attention and conveying complex information in a digestible format. Visual aids such as infographics, charts, and videos can make messages more engaging and memorable."

Mark, the head of engineering, spoke up. "How do we ensure that our visual communication is impactful?"

"We can invest in design resources or training to ensure that our visual communication is professional and effective," David replied. "By incorporating visuals into our communication strategy, we can create a more engaging and compelling experience for employees."

Sarah stood up, feeling a sense of determination and purpose. "Thank you, David. Effective internal communication is the cornerstone of a strong organizational culture. Let's commit to implementing strategies that foster transparency, collaboration, and engagement, ensuring that every employee feels informed, valued, and empowered to contribute to our success."

With their commitment to effective internal communication, the leadership team of Innovatech felt empowered to cultivate a culture of transparency, collaboration, and engagement. David felt a renewed sense of optimism and purpose for the journey ahead as they continued to prioritize communication in shaping the organization's culture.

The Role of Feedback in Cultural Development

In the collaborative atmosphere of Innovatech's meeting room, the leadership team delved into the vital role of feedback in shaping organizational culture. David Lawson understood that fostering a culture of continuous improvement and growth relied heavily on open and constructive feedback.

"Good morning, everyone," Sarah Mitchell, the CEO, greeted, her tone resonating with warmth and encouragement. "Today, we're exploring the critical role of feedback in cultural development. Feedback serves as a powerful tool for learning, growth, and alignment within the organization."

David nodded in agreement, his expression reflecting a deep appreciation for the transformative power of feedback. "Feedback enables us to identify strengths, address areas for improvement, and align individual and organizational goals, ultimately driving performance and success."

He clicked the remote, and a slide titled "The Role of Feedback in Cultural Development" appeared on the screen, outlining key points: Importance of Feedback Culture, Types of Feedback, Feedback Mechanisms, and Providing and Receiving Feedback Effectively.

"Let's start with the importance of a feedback culture," David began. "A feedback culture is characterized by open communication, trust, and a willingness to give and receive feedback at all levels of the organization. In a feedback-rich environment, employees feel empowered to share their perspectives, ideas, and concerns openly."

Tom, the HR manager, raised his hand. "How do we foster a feedback culture within our organization?"

"We can lead by example by soliciting and acting on feedback from employees," David suggested. "Leaders should encourage open dialogue, recognize and celebrate feedback, and create safe spaces for employees to share their thoughts and opinions without fear of judgment or reprisal."

Sarah nodded in agreement. "There are various types of feedback, including constructive feedback, positive reinforcement, and developmental feedback. Each type serves a different purpose in supporting employee growth and development."

Lisa, the marketing director, added, "Feedback mechanisms such as performance evaluations, 360-degree feedback, and regular check-ins provide opportunities for employees to receive feedback on their performance, progress, and development goals."

David smiled at her contribution. "Exactly, Lisa. By implementing diverse feedback mechanisms, we can ensure that employees receive timely and relevant feedback to support their growth and development."

He moved on to the next point. "Providing and receiving feedback effectively requires active listening, empathy, and openness. Employees should feel heard and understood, and feedback should be specific, actionable, and delivered with respect and sensitivity."

Mark, the head of engineering, spoke up. "How do we ensure that feedback is received and acted upon effectively?"

"We can establish processes and follow-up mechanisms to ensure that feedback is addressed and acted upon in a timely manner," David replied. "Leaders should provide support and resources to help employees implement feedback and make meaningful progress towards their goals."

Sarah stood up, feeling a sense of determination and purpose. "Thank you, David. Feedback is not just a tool for performance management; it's a catalyst for growth and cultural development. Let's commit to fostering a feedback culture where every employee feels valued, supported, and empowered to reach their full potential."

With their commitment to the role of feedback in cultural development, the leadership team of Innovatech felt empowered to cultivate a culture of continuous learning, improvement, and innovation. David felt a renewed sense of optimism and purpose for the journey ahead as they continued to prioritize feedback in shaping the organization's culture.

Building Open and Honest Communication Channels

In the collaborative ambiance of Innovatech's meeting room, the leadership team explored the essential role of building open and honest communication channels in shaping organizational culture. David Lawson understood that fostering an environment where employees feel comfortable expressing themselves openly is crucial for creating a culture of trust and transparency.

"Good morning, everyone," Sarah Mitchell, the CEO, greeted, her voice carrying a tone of inclusivity and encouragement. "Today, we're delving into the critical topic of building open and honest communication channels. Effective communication channels are the arteries of our organization, facilitating the flow of information, ideas, and feedback."

David nodded in agreement, his expression reflecting a deep understanding of the importance of fostering open communication. "Open and honest communication channels create a culture of trust, collaboration, and accountability, enabling employees to share their thoughts, concerns, and ideas without fear of judgment or reprisal."

He clicked the remote, and a slide titled "Building Open and Honest Communication Channels" appeared on the screen, outlining key points: Accessibility and Transparency, Diverse Communication Platforms, Regular Check-Ins, and Feedback Mechanisms.

"Let's start with accessibility and transparency," David began. "Leaders should make themselves accessible to employees, whether through open-door policies, regular town hall meetings, or informal check-ins. Transparency in communication builds trust and credibility, ensuring that employees feel informed and engaged."

Tom, the HR manager, raised his hand. "How do we ensure that our communication channels are accessible to all employees?"

"We can utilize diverse communication platforms to reach employees across different locations and departments," David suggested. "This may include email newsletters, intranet portals, digital signage, and social media groups. By leveraging multiple channels, we can ensure that information reaches everyone in a timely and accessible manner."

Sarah nodded in agreement. "Regular check-ins are also essential for fostering open communication. One-on-one meetings between managers and employees provide opportunities for dialogue, feedback, and coaching, strengthening relationships and alignment."

Lisa, the marketing director, added, "Feedback mechanisms such as suggestion boxes, surveys, and anonymous hotlines empower employees to voice their opinions, ideas, and concerns confidentially. Leaders should actively solicit feedback and act on it to demonstrate their commitment to open communication."

David smiled at her contribution. "Exactly, Lisa. By creating a culture where feedback is valued and acted upon, we foster a sense of ownership and accountability among employees."

He moved on to the next point. "Diverse communication platforms allow us to tailor our messaging to different audiences and preferences. Whether it's through written communications, visual presentations, or face-to-face interactions, we can ensure that our messages are clear, compelling, and engaging."

Mark, the head of engineering, spoke up. "How do we encourage employees to participate in communication channels and share their ideas and feedback?"

"We can lead by example by actively participating in communication channels and demonstrating openness and receptiveness to feedback," David replied. "Leaders should create a safe and supportive environment where employees feel encouraged and empowered to speak up and contribute to discussions."

Sarah stood up, feeling a sense of determination and purpose. "Thank you, David. Building open and honest communication channels is not just about disseminating information; it's about fostering a culture where every voice is heard, valued, and respected. Let's commit to creating an environment where communication flows freely, and ideas flourish."

With their commitment to building open and honest communication channels, the leadership team of Innovatech felt empowered to cultivate a culture of transparency, collaboration, and innovation. David felt a renewed sense of optimism and purpose for the journey ahead as they continued to prioritize communication in shaping the organization's culture.

Leveraging Technology for Better Communication

In the innovative atmosphere of Innovatech's meeting room, the leadership team explored the transformative power of leveraging technology for enhancing communication within the organization. David Lawson understood that embracing technology was essential for fostering efficiency, collaboration, and engagement in today's digital age.

"Good morning, everyone," Sarah Mitchell, the CEO, greeted, her voice infused with enthusiasm and anticipation. "Today, we're delving into the exciting topic of leveraging technology for better communication. Technology has the potential to revolutionize how we connect, collaborate, and communicate within our organization."

David nodded in agreement, his expression reflecting a keen interest in harnessing technology to drive organizational success. "Technology serves as a powerful enabler for breaking down barriers, facilitating real-time communication, and fostering a culture of innovation and agility."

He clicked the remote, and a slide titled "Leveraging Technology for Better Communication" appeared on the screen, outlining key points: Digital Collaboration Tools, Virtual Meeting Platforms, Mobile Applications, and Social Intranet Platforms.

"Let's start with digital collaboration tools," David began. "Collaboration tools such as Microsoft Teams, Slack, and Google Workspace enable real-time communication and collaboration, allowing employees to work together seamlessly regardless of their location or time zone."

Tom, the HR manager, raised his hand. "How do we ensure that our digital collaboration tools are effective and user-friendly?"

"We can involve employees in the selection and implementation process to ensure that the tools meet their needs and preferences," David suggested. "Training and support resources can also help employees become proficient in using the tools and maximize their benefits."

Sarah nodded in agreement. "Virtual meeting platforms such as Zoom, Microsoft Teams, and Webex enable face-to-face communication and collaboration, even when employees are geographically dispersed. These platforms facilitate team meetings, training sessions, and client presentations, fostering engagement and alignment."

Lisa, the marketing director, added, "Mobile applications allow employees to stay connected and access information on the go. Whether it's checking emails, reviewing documents, or participating in discussions, mobile apps provide flexibility and convenience for employees."

David smiled at her contribution. "Exactly, Lisa. By embracing mobile technology, we empower employees to work anytime, anywhere, and stay productive even outside the office."

He moved on to the next point. "Social intranet platforms such as Yammer, Workplace by Facebook, and Jive provide digital spaces for employees to connect, share knowledge, and collaborate. These platforms facilitate community-building, idea-sharing, and cross-departmental communication, fostering a sense of belonging and engagement."

Mark, the head of engineering, spoke up. "How do we ensure that technology enhances communication rather than detracts from it?"

"We can establish guidelines and best practices for using

technology effectively and respectfully," David replied. "Leaders should lead by example by embracing technology and modeling appropriate communication behaviors. By fostering a culture of digital literacy and etiquette, we can ensure that technology enhances communication and collaboration within the organization."

Sarah stood up, feeling a sense of determination and purpose. "Thank you, David. Leveraging technology for better communication is not just about adopting the latest tools; it's about embracing a mindset of innovation and adaptability. Let's commit to harnessing the power of technology to create a more connected, collaborative, and engaged workforce."

With their commitment to leveraging technology for better communication, the leadership team of Innovatech felt empowered to embrace digital transformation and drive organizational success in the digital age. David felt a renewed sense of optimism and purpose for the journey ahead as they continued to prioritize communication in shaping the organization's culture.

Addressing and Overcoming Communication Barriers

In the reflective ambiance of Innovatech's meeting room, the leadership team delved into the imperative task of addressing and overcoming communication barriers within the organization. David Lawson understood that identifying and addressing obstacles to communication was essential for fostering a culture of clarity, collaboration, and engagement.

"Good morning, everyone," Sarah Mitchell, the CEO, greeted, her voice filled with determination and resolve. "Today, we're tackling the crucial topic of addressing and overcoming communication barriers. Effective communication is the cornerstone of our organizational culture, and it's imperative that we identify and address any obstacles that hinder the flow of information and ideas."

David nodded in agreement, his expression reflecting a keen awareness of the challenges inherent in communication. "Communication barriers can take many forms, including language barriers, cultural differences, hierarchical structures, and technological limitations. It's essential that we proactively identify and address these barriers to ensure that communication flows freely and effectively within our organization."

He clicked the remote, and a slide titled "Addressing and Overcoming Communication Barriers" appeared on the screen, outlining key points: Cultural Awareness and Sensitivity, Clear and Concise Messaging, Active Listening, and Training and Development.

"Let's start with cultural awareness and sensitivity," David began. "Cultural differences can impact communication styles, preferences, and interpretations. By fostering cultural awareness and sensitivity among employees, we can ensure that communication is respectful, inclusive, and effective across diverse teams and stakeholders."

Tom, the HR manager, raised his hand. "How do we promote cultural awareness and sensitivity within our organization?"

"We can provide training and resources to help employees understand and appreciate cultural differences," David suggested. "Leaders should lead by example by demonstrating respect and openness to diverse perspectives. By fostering a culture of inclusivity and respect, we can create an environment where every voice is heard and valued."

Sarah nodded in agreement. "Clear and concise messaging

is also essential for overcoming communication barriers. Complex language, jargon, and ambiguity can impede understanding and create confusion. Leaders should strive to communicate clearly and concisely, using plain language and avoiding unnecessary complexity."

Lisa, the marketing director, added, "Active listening is equally important for effective communication. Employees should feel heard and understood, and leaders should demonstrate empathy and attentiveness when listening to their concerns and ideas."

David smiled at her contribution. "Exactly, Lisa. By practicing active listening, we can build trust and rapport with employees, fostering open and honest communication."

He moved on to the next point. "Training and development programs can also help employees develop their communication skills and overcome barriers. Whether it's through workshops, coaching, or e-learning modules, investing in communication training can empower employees to communicate more effectively and confidently."

Mark, the head of engineering, spoke up. "How do we ensure that our training programs are effective and impactful?"

"We can tailor training programs to meet the specific needs and preferences of employees," David replied. "Interactive and practical exercises can help employees apply their learning to real-world situations, while feedback and coaching can provide guidance and support for continuous improvement."

Sarah stood up, feeling a sense of determination and purpose. "Thank you, David. Addressing and overcoming communication barriers is not just about removing obstacles; it's about fostering a culture of understanding, collaboration, and respect. Let's commit to creating an environment where communication flows freely, and every voice is heard and valued."

With their commitment to addressing and overcoming communication barriers, the leadership team of Innovatech felt empowered to create a more inclusive, collaborative, and effective communication environment. David felt a renewed sense of optimism and purpose for the journey ahead as they continued to prioritize communication in shaping the organization's culture.

Case Studies of Successful Communication Practices

In the vibrant atmosphere of Innovatech's meeting room, the leadership team embarked on an exploration of successful communication practices through insightful case studies. David Lawson understood the value of learning from real-world examples to inspire and inform their communication strategies.

"Good morning, everyone," Sarah Mitchell, the CEO, greeted, her voice resonating with eagerness and curiosity. "Today, we're diving into the fascinating world of successful communication practices through case studies. By examining real-world examples of effective communication, we can glean valuable insights and inspiration for enhancing our own communication efforts."

David nodded in agreement, his expression reflecting a keen interest in uncovering actionable lessons from the experiences of other organizations. "Case studies provide us with tangible examples of how effective communication can drive engagement, alignment, and success within organizations."

He clicked the remote, and a slide titled "Case Studies of

Successful Communication Practices" appeared on the screen, showcasing examples from various industries and contexts.

"Let's start with the case study of Company X," David began. "Company X implemented a transparent communication strategy that included regular town hall meetings, open-door policies, and digital communication platforms. By fostering transparency and accessibility, Company X created a culture where employees felt informed, valued, and engaged."

Tom, the HR manager, raised his hand. "How did Company X ensure that their communication strategy was effective?"

"Company X solicited feedback from employees through surveys, focus groups, and feedback mechanisms," David replied. "They used this feedback to refine their communication channels and messages, ensuring that they met the needs and preferences of employees."

Sarah nodded in agreement. "Another inspiring case study is the communication approach of Company Y during a period of organizational change. Company Y proactively communicated with employees about the reasons for change, the impact on their roles, and the support available to them. By providing clear and consistent communication, Company Y minimized uncertainty and resistance, fostering a smoother transition and maintaining employee morale."

Lisa, the marketing director, added, "Company Z is another excellent example of effective communication practices. They implemented a digital communication platform that facilitated real-time collaboration, knowledge sharing, and community-building among employees. By leveraging technology, Company Z created a more connected and engaged workforce, leading to increased productivity and innovation."

David smiled at her contribution. "Exactly, Lisa. These case studies highlight the power of effective communication in driving employee engagement, alignment, and organizational success. By learning from these examples, we can identify strategies and best practices to enhance our own communication efforts."

He moved on to the next case study. "Lastly, let's explore the communication approach of Company W during a crisis situation. Company W demonstrated leadership transparency, empathy, and authenticity in their communication with employees and stakeholders. By providing regular updates, acknowledging concerns, and offering support, Company W built trust and confidence, helping the organization navigate through the crisis with resilience and unity."

Mark, the head of engineering, spoke up. "How can we apply the lessons from these case studies to our own communication efforts?"

"We can identify common themes and strategies from these case studies and adapt them to our own organizational context," David suggested. "Whether it's fostering transparency, soliciting feedback, leveraging technology, or demonstrating empathy, we can draw inspiration from these examples to enhance our communication practices and create a culture where communication thrives."

Sarah stood up, feeling a sense of inspiration and motivation. "Thank you, David. Case studies of successful communication practices provide valuable insights and inspiration for improving our own communication efforts. Let's commit to learning from these examples and applying their lessons to create a culture of clarity, collaboration, and engagement within our organization."

With their commitment to learning from successful communication practices, the leadership team of Innovatech felt empowered to elevate their communication efforts and drive positive change within the organization. David felt a renewed sense of optimism and purpose for the journey ahead as they continued to prioritize communication in shaping the organization's culture.

6

Chapter 6: Diversity, Equity, and Inclusion

Defining Diversity, Equity, and Inclusion (DEI)

In the inclusive atmosphere of Innovatech's meeting room, the leadership team embarked on a journey to explore the fundamental concepts of diversity, equity, and inclusion. David Lawson understood that embracing diversity and fostering a culture of equity and inclusion was essential for driving innovation, creativity, and organizational success.

"Good morning, everyone," Sarah Mitchell, the CEO, greeted, her voice infused with warmth and conviction. "Today, we're delving into the crucial topic of diversity, equity, and inclusion (DEI). DEI is not just a buzzword; it's a guiding principle that shapes how we operate as an organization and as individuals."

David nodded in agreement, his expression reflecting a deep commitment to championing DEI within the organization. "Diversity encompasses the range of differences among individuals, including but not limited to race, ethnicity, gender, sexual orientation, age, disability, religion, and socio-economic background."

He clicked the remote, and a slide titled "Defining Diversity, Equity, and Inclusion (DEI)" appeared on the screen, outlining key points: Diversity, Equity, Inclusion, and Intersectionality.

"Let's start with diversity," David began. "Diversity is about recognizing, valuing, and celebrating the unique perspectives, experiences, and identities that each individual brings to the table. It's about creating a workforce that reflects the rich tapestry of humanity and harnessing the power of diverse voices and ideas to drive innovation and growth."

Tom, the HR manager, raised his hand. "How do we ensure that our organization embraces diversity in all its forms?"

"We can foster diversity by actively recruiting and retaining employees from diverse backgrounds and perspectives," David replied. "This includes implementing inclusive hiring practices, providing equal opportunities for advancement and development, and creating a supportive and inclusive work environment where all employees feel valued and respected."

Sarah nodded in agreement. "Equity is the next pillar of DEI. Equity is about ensuring fairness and justice in the treatment of all individuals, regardless of their background or identity. It's about recognizing and addressing systemic barriers and inequities that prevent certain groups from fully participating and thriving within the organization."

Lisa, the marketing director, added, "Inclusion is the final piece of the puzzle. Inclusion is about creating a sense of belonging and community where all individuals feel welcomed, respected, and valued for who they are. It's about fostering an environment where diverse perspectives are heard, valued, and integrated into decision-making and problem-solving processes."

David smiled at her contribution. "Exactly, Lisa. Inclusion is not just about diversity; it's about leveraging diversity to create a culture of belonging and empowerment for all employees."

He moved on to the next point. "Intersectionality is another important aspect of DEI. Intersectionality recognizes that individuals hold multiple social identities that intersect and interact with each other, shaping their experiences and perspectives. By understanding and addressing the intersectionality of identity, we can ensure that our DEI efforts are inclusive and equitable for all individuals."

Mark, the head of engineering, spoke up. "How do we translate these concepts into actionable strategies within our organization?"

"We can start by embedding DEI principles into our policies, practices, and culture," David suggested. "This includes implementing diversity training and education programs, establishing diversity and inclusion councils or committees, and setting measurable goals and accountability mechanisms to track our progress towards building a more diverse, equitable, and inclusive organization."

Sarah stood up, feeling a sense of determination and purpose. "Thank you, David. Defining diversity, equity, and inclusion (DEI) is just the beginning of our journey towards creating a more equitable and inclusive organization. Let's commit to embracing diversity, promoting equity, and fostering inclusion in everything we do, both within our organization and in the broader community."

With their commitment to diversity, equity, and inclusion, the leadership team of Innovatech felt empowered to create a more equitable, inclusive, and vibrant workplace. David felt a renewed sense of optimism and purpose for the journey ahead as they continued to prioritize DEI in shaping the organization's culture.

The Benefits of a Diverse Workforce

In the inclusive setting of Innovatech's meeting room, the leadership team delved deeper into the advantages of fostering a diverse workforce. David Lawson recognized that embracing diversity not only cultivates a vibrant organizational culture but also drives innovation, creativity, and business success.

"Good morning, everyone," Sarah Mitchell, the CEO, greeted, her voice resonating with enthusiasm and optimism. "Today, we're exploring the myriad benefits of having a diverse workforce. Diversity is not just a moral imperative; it's a strategic advantage that fuels our organization's growth and success."

David nodded in agreement, his expression reflecting a deep understanding of the transformative power of diversity. "A diverse workforce brings a wealth of perspectives, experiences, and ideas to the table. By embracing diversity, we tap into a rich reservoir of creativity, innovation, and problem-solving capabilities."

He clicked the remote, and a slide titled "The Benefits of a Diverse Workforce" appeared on the screen, outlining key points: Innovation and Creativity, Better Decision-Making, Enhanced Customer Understanding, and Improved Employee Engagement.

"Let's start with innovation and creativity," David began. "Research has consistently shown that diverse teams are more innovative and creative. By bringing together individuals with different backgrounds, skills, and perspectives, we foster a culture of collaboration, exploration, and experimentation, leading to breakthrough ideas and solutions."

Tom, the HR manager, raised his hand. "How does diversity contribute to innovation and creativity?"

"Diversity encourages divergent thinking and challenges groupthink," David replied. "When individuals with different perspectives come together, they are more likely to question assumptions, challenge conventional wisdom, and approach problems from multiple angles. This diversity of thought sparks creativity and drives innovation."

Sarah nodded in agreement. "Better decision-making is another key benefit of diversity. Diverse teams are better equipped to anticipate risks, identify opportunities, and make informed decisions. By considering a wide range of perspectives and viewpoints, we arrive at more robust and well-rounded decisions that drive business success."

Lisa, the marketing director, added, "Enhanced customer understanding is also a critical advantage of diversity. A diverse workforce mirrors the diversity of our customer base, allowing us to better understand their needs, preferences, and experiences. This deep understanding enables us to tailor our products, services, and marketing strategies to meet the diverse needs of our customers."

David smiled at her contribution. "Exactly, Lisa. By embracing diversity, we build stronger connections with our customers and enhance our competitiveness in the market."

He moved on to the next point. "Improved employee engagement is yet another benefit of diversity. When employees feel valued, respected, and included, they are more engaged, motivated, and committed to the organization's goals and success. Diversity fosters a culture of belonging and empowerment, where every employee feels valued and respected for who they are."

Mark, the head of engineering, spoke up. "How do we ensure that we maximize the benefits of a diverse workforce?"

"We can create an inclusive culture where diversity is celebrated and valued," David suggested. "This includes providing training and education on diversity and inclusion, establishing mentorship and sponsorship programs for underrepresented groups, and setting clear expectations and accountability mechanisms for promoting diversity and inclusion at all levels of the organization."

Sarah stood up, feeling a sense of inspiration and purpose. "Thank you, David. The benefits of a diverse workforce are clear and compelling. Let's commit to embracing diversity, fostering inclusion, and leveraging the full potential of our diverse team to drive innovation, creativity, and business success."

With their commitment to the benefits of a diverse workforce, the leadership team of Innovatech felt empowered to create a more inclusive, innovative, and successful organization. David felt a renewed sense of optimism and purpose for the journey ahead as they continued to prioritize diversity and inclusion in shaping the organization's culture.

Strategies for Promoting DEI

In the inclusive ambiance of Innovatech's meeting room, the leadership team delved into actionable strategies for promoting diversity, equity, and inclusion (DEI) within the organization. David Lawson recognized that implementing effective strategies was essential for translating their commitment to DEI into

CHAPTER 6: DIVERSITY, EQUITY, AND INCLUSION

tangible outcomes.

"Good morning, everyone," Sarah Mitchell, the CEO, greeted, her voice filled with determination and purpose. "Today, we're diving into the vital topic of strategies for promoting diversity, equity, and inclusion (DEI). DEI is not just a goal; it's a journey that requires intentional effort and dedication."

David nodded in agreement, his expression reflecting a steadfast commitment to driving DEI initiatives within the organization. "Promoting DEI requires a multifaceted approach that addresses systemic barriers, fosters inclusive practices, and promotes a culture of belonging and respect."

He clicked the remote, and a slide titled "Strategies for Promoting DEI" appeared on the screen, outlining key points: Inclusive Recruitment Practices, Diversity Training and Education, Bias Awareness and Mitigation, and Supportive Policies and Practices.

"Let's start with inclusive recruitment practices," David began. "Recruitment is the first step in building a diverse workforce. We can promote diversity by implementing inclusive hiring practices, such as removing biases from job descriptions, utilizing diverse sourcing channels, and implementing blind resume screening techniques to focus on skills and qualifications rather than demographic factors."

Tom, the HR manager, raised his hand. "How can we ensure that our recruitment process is inclusive and equitable?"

"We can establish diversity goals and metrics to track our progress and hold ourselves accountable," David suggested. "We can also provide unconscious bias training for hiring managers and interviewers to raise awareness of biases and mitigate their impact on hiring decisions."

Sarah nodded in agreement. "Diversity training and education are also essential for promoting DEI. By providing training on topics such as unconscious bias, cultural competency, and inclusive leadership, we can increase awareness and understanding of DEI issues and empower employees to contribute to a more inclusive workplace."

Lisa, the marketing director, added, "Bias awareness and mitigation is another critical aspect of promoting DEI. We can implement processes and tools to identify and address biases in decision-making processes, such as performance evaluations, promotions, and resource allocation."

David smiled at her contribution. "Exactly, Lisa. By fostering a culture of transparency and accountability, we can ensure that our decisions are fair, equitable, and free from bias."

He moved on to the next point. "Supportive policies and practices are also essential for promoting DEI. We can implement policies and practices that support work-life balance, flexibility, and inclusion, such as flexible work arrangements, parental leave policies, and diversity and inclusion councils or committees."

Mark, the head of engineering, spoke up. "How can we ensure that our policies and practices are inclusive and equitable?"

"We can involve employees in the development and review of policies and practices to ensure that they reflect the needs and perspectives of diverse individuals," David replied. "We can also provide resources and support for employees from underrepresented groups to ensure that they have equal opportunities for advancement and development."

Sarah stood up, feeling a sense of determination and purpose. "Thank you, David. Strategies for promoting DEI are essential for creating a more inclusive, equitable, and vibrant workplace. Let's commit to implementing these strategies and fostering a culture where diversity, equity, and inclusion thrive."

With their commitment to promoting DEI, the leadership team of Innovatech felt empowered to drive positive change and create a more inclusive and equitable organization. David felt a renewed sense of optimism and purpose for the journey ahead as they continued to prioritize DEI in shaping the organization's culture.

Addressing Unconscious Bias

In the enlightened atmosphere of Innovatech's meeting room, the leadership team delved into the critical task of addressing unconscious bias within the organization. David Lawson recognized that unconscious bias could hinder efforts to foster diversity, equity, and inclusion (DEI) and was determined to confront it head-on.

"Good morning, everyone," Sarah Mitchell, the CEO, greeted, her voice filled with determination and resolve. "Today, we're tackling the important topic of addressing unconscious bias. Unconscious bias can influence our decisions and behaviors in subtle ways, and it's essential that we confront and mitigate its impact to create a more equitable and inclusive workplace."

David nodded in agreement, his expression reflecting a deep understanding of the pervasive nature of unconscious bias. "Unconscious bias refers to the automatic, unintentional preferences or stereotypes that influence our perceptions, judgments, and behaviors. While often subtle and unconscious, these biases can have profound effects on our interactions and decision-making processes."

He clicked the remote, and a slide titled "Addressing Unconscious Bias" appeared on the screen, outlining key points:

Awareness and Recognition, Training and Education, Mitigation Strategies, and Accountability.

"Let's start with awareness and recognition," David began. "The first step in addressing unconscious bias is to raise awareness of its existence and impact. By educating ourselves and others about the nature of unconscious bias and its effects on decision-making, we can begin to recognize and challenge our own biases."

Tom, the HR manager, raised his hand. "How can we raise awareness of unconscious bias within our organization?"

"We can provide training and education on unconscious bias for all employees, from frontline staff to senior leaders," David suggested. "These training programs can help employees understand the different types of biases, recognize their own biases, and learn strategies for mitigating bias in their decision-making processes."

Sarah nodded in agreement. "Training and education are essential for building a culture of awareness and accountability around unconscious bias. By providing employees with the knowledge and tools to recognize and address bias, we empower them to contribute to a more inclusive and equitable workplace."

Lisa, the marketing director, added, "Mitigation strategies are another critical aspect of addressing unconscious bias. We can implement processes and tools to minimize bias in decision-making processes, such as standardized hiring criteria, diverse hiring panels, and structured interview formats."

David smiled at her contribution. "Exactly, Lisa. By implementing these strategies, we can create a more fair and equitable workplace where decisions are based on merit and qualifications rather than unconscious biases."

He moved on to the next point. "Accountability is also essential for addressing unconscious bias. We can establish clear expectations and accountability mechanisms for addressing bias, such as incorporating bias awareness into performance evaluations and providing feedback and coaching for biased behavior."

Mark, the head of engineering, spoke up. "How can we ensure that our efforts to address unconscious bias are effective and impactful?"

"We can regularly evaluate and assess the effectiveness of our unconscious bias training and mitigation strategies," David replied. "This may include soliciting feedback from employees, tracking key metrics related to diversity and inclusion, and making adjustments to our programs and practices as needed."

Sarah stood up, feeling a sense of determination and purpose. "Thank you, David. Addressing unconscious bias is essential for creating a more inclusive and equitable workplace. Let's commit to raising awareness, providing training and education, implementing mitigation strategies, and holding ourselves accountable for addressing bias in all its forms."

With their commitment to addressing unconscious bias, the leadership team of Innovatech felt empowered to create a more fair, inclusive, and equitable organization. David felt a renewed sense of optimism and purpose for the journey ahead as they continued to prioritize DEI in shaping the organization's culture.

Creating Inclusive Policies and Practices

In the progressive ambiance of Innovatech's meeting room, the leadership team delved into the pivotal task of creating inclusive policies and practices within the organization. David Lawson understood that embedding inclusivity into policies and practices was essential for fostering a culture of diversity, equity, and inclusion (DEI).

"Good morning, everyone," Sarah Mitchell, the CEO, greeted, her voice brimming with determination and purpose. "Today, we're focusing on the critical topic of creating inclusive policies and practices. Inclusivity is not just a buzzword; it's a fundamental value that should be reflected in everything we do as an organization."

David nodded in agreement, his expression reflecting a deep commitment to promoting inclusivity within the organization. "Creating inclusive policies and practices is essential for ensuring that all employees feel valued, respected, and empowered to contribute to their fullest potential."

He clicked the remote, and a slide titled "Creating Inclusive Policies and Practices" appeared on the screen, outlining key points: Diversity and Inclusion Committees, Flexible Work Arrangements, Diversity Training, and Inclusive Benefits.

"Let's start with diversity and inclusion committees," David began. "Diversity and inclusion committees play a crucial role in driving DEI initiatives within the organization. These committees, comprised of representatives from diverse backgrounds and departments, can provide valuable insights, guidance, and accountability for DEI efforts."

Tom, the HR manager, raised his hand. "How can we ensure that our diversity and inclusion committees are effective and impactful?"

"We can empower these committees with clear mandates, resources, and support from senior leadership," David suggested. "They can be tasked with developing and implementing DEI initiatives, providing feedback and recommendations on policies and practices, and fostering a culture of inclusivity and belonging within their respective departments."

Sarah nodded in agreement. "Flexible work arrangements are another essential component of creating an inclusive workplace. By offering flexible work options, such as remote work, flexible hours, and compressed workweeks, we can accommodate the diverse needs and preferences of our employees and promote work-life balance."

Lisa, the marketing director, added, "Diversity training is also critical for creating an inclusive workplace culture. By providing training on topics such as unconscious bias, cultural competency, and inclusive leadership, we can increase awareness and understanding of DEI issues and empower employees to contribute to a more inclusive environment."

David smiled at her contribution. "Exactly, Lisa. Diversity training helps employees recognize and challenge their own biases, develop empathy and cultural competence, and learn strategies for promoting diversity and inclusion in their daily interactions and decision-making processes."

He moved on to the next point. "Inclusive benefits are another important aspect of creating an inclusive workplace. By offering benefits that meet the diverse needs of our employees and their families, such as parental leave, childcare support, and mental health resources, we can create a more supportive and inclusive environment where all employees feel valued and supported."

Mark, the head of engineering, spoke up. "How can we ensure that our policies and practices are inclusive and equitable?"

"We can involve employees in the development and review of policies and practices to ensure that they reflect the needs and perspectives of diverse individuals," David replied. "We can also regularly evaluate and assess the impact of our policies and practices on diversity and inclusion and make adjustments as needed to ensure that they are equitable and effective."

Sarah stood up, feeling a sense of determination and purpose. "Thank you, David. Creating inclusive policies and practices is essential for fostering a culture where diversity, equity, and inclusion thrive. Let's commit to embedding inclusivity into everything we do and creating a workplace where every employee feels valued, respected, and empowered to succeed."

With their commitment to creating inclusive policies and practices, the leadership team of Innovatech felt empowered to drive positive change and create a more inclusive and equitable organization. David felt a renewed sense of optimism and purpose for the journey ahead as they continued to prioritize DEI in shaping the organization's culture.

Measuring DEI Progress and Impact

In the forward-thinking atmosphere of Innovatech's meeting room, the leadership team delved into the essential task of measuring diversity, equity, and inclusion (DEI) progress and impact within the organization. David Lawson understood that establishing metrics and accountability mechanisms was crucial for evaluating the effectiveness of their DEI initiatives.

"Good morning, everyone," Sarah Mitchell, the CEO, greeted, her voice filled with determination and purpose. "Today, we're

CHAPTER 6: DIVERSITY, EQUITY, AND INCLUSION

focusing on the vital topic of measuring DEI progress and impact. If we want to create a truly inclusive organization, we need to be able to track our progress and understand the impact of our efforts."

David nodded in agreement, his expression reflecting a deep commitment to transparency and accountability in DEI efforts. "Measuring DEI progress and impact allows us to identify areas of strength, areas for improvement, and opportunities for growth. It also helps us hold ourselves accountable for making meaningful and lasting change."

He clicked the remote, and a slide titled "Measuring DEI Progress and Impact" appeared on the screen, outlining key points: Key Performance Indicators (KPIs), Employee Surveys, Diversity Dashboards, and External Benchmarks.

"Let's start with key performance indicators (KPIs)," David began. "KPIs are measurable objectives that allow us to track our progress towards specific DEI goals. These may include metrics such as workforce diversity representation, employee turnover rates, promotion and advancement rates by demographic group, and employee engagement and satisfaction scores."

Tom, the HR manager, raised his hand. "How do we establish meaningful KPIs for DEI?"

"We can start by identifying our organization's DEI priorities and goals," David suggested. "These may include increasing diversity representation at all levels of the organization, reducing turnover rates for underrepresented groups, or improving employee satisfaction and engagement scores among diverse employees. Once we've identified our priorities, we can develop KPIs that align with these goals and allow us to track our progress over time."

Sarah nodded in agreement. "Employee surveys are another valuable tool for measuring DEI progress and impact. By soliciting feedback from employees on their perceptions and experiences related to diversity, equity, and inclusion, we can gain valuable insights into areas of strength and areas for improvement."

Lisa, the marketing director, added, "Diversity dashboards are also helpful for visualizing and tracking DEI metrics in real-time. These dashboards can provide a snapshot of workforce demographics, diversity representation in leadership roles, and progress towards DEI goals, allowing us to identify trends and patterns and make data-driven decisions."

David smiled at her contribution. "Exactly, Lisa. By leveraging technology and data analytics, we can gain deeper insights into our DEI efforts and identify areas where we need to focus our attention."

He moved on to the next point. "External benchmarks are another valuable resource for measuring DEI progress and impact. By comparing our organization's DEI metrics to industry benchmarks and best practices, we can gain a broader perspective on our performance and identify areas where we can learn and improve."

Mark, the head of engineering, spoke up. "How can we ensure that we're using these metrics effectively to drive meaningful change?"

"We can establish regular review processes to assess our progress against our DEI goals and identify opportunities for improvement," David replied. "This may include quarterly or annual reviews of DEI metrics, discussions with key stakeholders to evaluate the effectiveness of our initiatives, and adjustments to our strategies and action plans as needed."

CHAPTER 6: DIVERSITY, EQUITY, AND INCLUSION

Sarah stood up, feeling a sense of determination and purpose. "Thank you, David. Measuring DEI progress and impact is essential for holding ourselves accountable and driving meaningful change. Let's commit to using these metrics to guide our DEI efforts and create a more inclusive and equitable organization."

With their commitment to measuring DEI progress and impact, the leadership team of Innovatech felt empowered to drive positive change and create a more inclusive and equitable organization. David felt a renewed sense of optimism and purpose for the journey ahead as they continued to prioritize DEI in shaping the organization's culture.

Chapter 7: Developing and Sustaining Culture

Strategies for Cultural Change and Transformation

In the dynamic atmosphere of Innovatech's meeting room, the leadership team embarked on a journey to explore strategies for cultural change and transformation within the organization. David Lawson understood that developing and sustaining a positive organizational culture was essential for driving performance, engagement, and success.

"Good morning, everyone," Sarah Mitchell, the CEO, greeted, her voice infused with energy and enthusiasm. "Today, we're diving into the exciting topic of strategies for cultural change and transformation. Cultivating a vibrant and inclusive culture is not just about what we say; it's about what we do and how we do it."

David nodded in agreement, his expression reflecting a deep commitment to fostering a culture of excellence and innovation within the organization. "Strategies for cultural change and transformation are essential for aligning our values, behaviors, and practices with our desired organizational culture."

He clicked the remote, and a slide titled "Strategies for Cultural Change and Transformation" appeared on the screen, outlining key points: Vision and Alignment, Leadership Commitment, Employee Involvement, Continuous Learning, and Celebrating Successes.

"Let's start with vision and alignment," David began. "Vision and alignment are the foundation of cultural change and transformation. We need to clearly articulate our desired culture, values, and behaviors and ensure that they are aligned with our organizational goals and objectives."

Tom, the HR manager, raised his hand. "How can we ensure that our vision and values are effectively communicated and understood by all employees?"

"We can involve employees in the development of our vision and values to ensure that they reflect the aspirations and beliefs of the entire organization," David suggested. "We can also communicate our vision and values regularly through various channels, such as town hall meetings, newsletters, and employee forums, and ensure that they are integrated into all aspects of our organization's operations and decision-making processes."

Sarah nodded in agreement. "Leadership commitment is another essential element of cultural change and transformation. Leaders play a critical role in setting the tone, modeling behaviors, and reinforcing desired cultural norms and expectations."

Lisa, the marketing director, added, "Employee involvement is also key to driving cultural change and transformation. By involving employees in decision-making processes, soliciting their feedback and ideas, and empowering them to take ownership of the culture, we can create a sense of ownership and commitment to our cultural journey."

David smiled at her contribution. "Exactly, Lisa. By fostering a culture of collaboration and participation, we can harness the collective wisdom and creativity of our employees to drive meaningful change."

He moved on to the next point. "Continuous learning is essential for sustaining cultural change and transformation. We need to provide employees with opportunities for growth, development, and learning, such as training programs, workshops, and mentorship opportunities, to ensure that they have the skills and capabilities to thrive in our evolving culture."

Mark, the head of engineering, spoke up. "How can we ensure that our employees are engaged and motivated to participate in our cultural transformation efforts?"

"We can recognize and celebrate successes along the way," David replied. "By acknowledging and rewarding employees who demonstrate our desired cultural values and behaviors, we reinforce the importance of our cultural journey and inspire others to join us on the path to cultural excellence."

Sarah stood up, feeling a sense of excitement and purpose. "Thank you, David. Strategies for cultural change and transformation are essential for shaping the future of our organization. Let's commit to aligning our vision, engaging our employees, and celebrating our successes as we embark on this transformative journey together."

With their commitment to strategies for cultural change and transformation, the leadership team of Innovatech felt empowered to drive positive change and create a culture of excellence and innovation within the organization. David felt a renewed sense of optimism and purpose for the journey ahead as they continued to prioritize cultural development and sustainability.

The Role of Training and Development

In the vibrant atmosphere of Innovatech's meeting room, the leadership team delved into the crucial role of training and development in shaping organizational culture. David Lawson understood that investing in employee growth and learning was essential for fostering a culture of continuous improvement and innovation.

"Good morning, everyone," Sarah Mitchell, the CEO, greeted, her voice brimming with enthusiasm and determination. "Today, we're exploring the pivotal role of training and development in developing and sustaining our organizational culture. Investing in our employees' growth and learning is not just an investment in their future; it's an investment in the future of our organization."

David nodded in agreement, his expression reflecting a deep commitment to nurturing talent and building a culture of excellence within the organization. "Training and development play a crucial role in equipping our employees with the knowledge, skills, and capabilities they need to thrive in our evolving culture."

He clicked the remote, and a slide titled "The Role of Training and Development" appeared on the screen, outlining key points: Skill Enhancement, Cultural Alignment, Leadership Development, and Continuous Learning.

"Let's start with skill enhancement," David began. "Skill

enhancement is essential for ensuring that our employees have the technical, interpersonal, and leadership skills they need to succeed in their roles and contribute to our organizational goals. By providing targeted training and development programs, we can help employees acquire new skills, refine existing ones, and stay ahead of industry trends and best practices."

Tom, the HR manager, raised his hand. "How can we ensure that our training programs are aligned with our organizational culture?"

"We can tailor our training programs to reinforce our organizational values, behaviors, and expectations," David suggested. "For example, if collaboration is one of our core values, we can offer training programs on teamwork, communication, and conflict resolution. By aligning our training initiatives with our cultural priorities, we can reinforce desired behaviors and foster a culture of excellence."

Sarah nodded in agreement. "Leadership development is another critical aspect of training and development. Our leaders play a key role in shaping our organizational culture and setting the tone for our employees. By investing in leadership development programs, we can equip our leaders with the skills, knowledge, and mindset they need to inspire and empower their teams, drive performance, and champion our cultural values."

Lisa, the marketing director, added, "Continuous learning is essential for staying agile and adaptive in today's rapidly changing business landscape. By fostering a culture of continuous learning and development, we can encourage employees to seek out new opportunities for growth, experiment with new ideas and approaches, and embrace lifelong learning as a core value."

David smiled at her contribution. "Exactly, Lisa. By providing employees with access to a variety of learning resources and opportunities, such as online courses, workshops, mentorship programs, and leadership development initiatives, we can create a culture where curiosity, growth, and innovation thrive."

He moved on to the next point. "Measuring the impact of our training and development initiatives is essential for ensuring that we're achieving our desired outcomes and driving meaningful change. We can track key metrics such as employee satisfaction, engagement, retention, and performance to evaluate the effectiveness of our programs and make data-driven decisions to continuously improve and refine our training and development efforts."

Mark, the head of engineering, spoke up. "How can we ensure that our training and development programs are accessible and inclusive for all employees?"

"We can provide a variety of learning opportunities and formats to accommodate different learning styles, preferences, and needs," David replied. "This may include offering both in-person and virtual training options, providing captioning or transcripts for training materials, and ensuring that training content is culturally relevant and inclusive. By prioritizing accessibility and inclusion in our training and development programs, we can ensure that all employees have the opportunity to learn, grow, and succeed."

Sarah stood up, feeling a sense of excitement and purpose. "Thank you, David. The role of training and development is pivotal in shaping our organizational culture and driving our success. Let's commit to investing in our employees' growth and learning as we continue to build a culture of excellence, innovation, and inclusion."

With their commitment to the role of training and development, the leadership team of Innovatech felt empowered to nurture talent, drive performance, and sustain a culture of continuous improvement within the organization. David felt a renewed sense of optimism and purpose for the journey ahead as they continued to prioritize employee development and organizational excellence.

Embedding Culture in Policies and Procedures

In the purposeful atmosphere of Innovatech's meeting room, the leadership team delved into the vital task of embedding culture in policies and procedures within the organization. David Lawson understood that aligning policies and procedures with the desired organizational culture was essential for fostering consistency, accountability, and alignment with core values.

"Good morning, everyone," Sarah Mitchell, the CEO, greeted, her voice filled with determination and resolve. "Today, we're exploring the critical topic of embedding culture in policies and procedures. Our policies and procedures are more than just rules; they're a reflection of our values, beliefs, and expectations as an organization."

David nodded in agreement, his expression reflecting a deep understanding of the importance of aligning policies and procedures with the organizational culture. "Embedding culture in policies and procedures is essential for ensuring that our values and expectations are consistently reinforced and upheld across the organization."

He clicked the remote, and a slide titled "Embedding Culture

CHAPTER 7: DEVELOPING AND SUSTAINING CULTURE

in Policies and Procedures" appeared on the screen, outlining key points: Values Alignment, Transparency, Accountability, and Flexibility.

"Let's start with values alignment," David began. "Our policies and procedures should be aligned with our organizational values, beliefs, and priorities. For example, if innovation is one of our core values, our policies should encourage experimentation, risk-taking, and creativity. By aligning our policies with our values, we ensure that our actions are consistent with our cultural aspirations."

Tom, the HR manager, raised his hand. "How can we ensure that our policies and procedures reflect our organizational values?"

"We can involve employees in the development and review of our policies and procedures to ensure that they align with our cultural priorities," David suggested. "This may include soliciting feedback through surveys, focus groups, or town hall meetings, and incorporating employee input into the design and implementation of our policies. By involving employees in the process, we can ensure that our policies reflect the diverse perspectives and experiences of our workforce."

Sarah nodded in agreement. "Transparency is another essential element of embedding culture in policies and procedures. Our policies should be clear, accessible, and easy to understand, and employees should have the opportunity to provide feedback, ask questions, and seek clarification when needed. By fostering transparency in our policies and procedures, we build trust and confidence among our employees and reinforce our commitment to openness and integrity."

Lisa, the marketing director, added, "Accountability is also crucial for embedding culture in policies and procedures. Our policies should establish clear expectations, standards, and consequences for behavior, and employees should be held accountable for upholding our cultural values and meeting performance expectations. By holding ourselves and others accountable, we create a culture of responsibility, fairness, and equity."

David smiled at her contribution. "Exactly, Lisa. Flexibility is another important aspect of embedding culture in policies and procedures. While it's essential to establish guidelines and standards, we also need to allow for flexibility and adaptability to accommodate different situations, contexts, and individual needs. By providing employees with the autonomy and flexibility to make decisions and solve problems in alignment with our cultural values, we empower them to contribute to our organizational success."

He moved on to the next point. "Measuring the impact of our policies and procedures is essential for ensuring that they are effective in reinforcing our cultural values and driving desired behaviors. We can track key metrics such as employee compliance, satisfaction, and engagement to evaluate the effectiveness of our policies and procedures and make adjustments as needed to ensure that they are aligned with our cultural aspirations."

Mark, the head of engineering, spoke up. "How can we ensure that our policies and procedures are consistently applied and enforced across the organization?"

"We can provide training and resources to ensure that employees understand our policies and procedures and their role in upholding our cultural values," David replied. "We can also establish mechanisms for monitoring and enforcement to ensure that our policies are consistently applied and enforced, and employees are held accountable for their actions. By fostering a culture of compliance and accountability, we create a safe, fair, and inclusive work environment where everyone can thrive."

Sarah stood up, feeling a sense of satisfaction and purpose. "Thank you, David. Embedding culture in policies and procedures is essential for shaping our organizational identity and driving our success. Let's commit to aligning our policies with our values, fostering transparency and accountability, and promoting flexibility and adaptability as we continue to build a culture of excellence, integrity, and innovation."

With their commitment to embedding culture in policies and procedures, the leadership team of Innovatech felt empowered to shape organizational practices and norms in alignment with their cultural aspirations. David felt a renewed sense of optimism and purpose for the journey ahead as they continued to prioritize cultural development and sustainability.

Maintaining Culture Through Growth and Change

In the focused ambiance of Innovatech's meeting room, the leadership team delved into the crucial task of maintaining culture through growth and change within the organization. David Lawson understood that preserving the core values and identity of the organization was essential for sustaining a cohesive and thriving culture, especially during periods of expansion or transformation.

"Good morning, everyone," Sarah Mitchell, the CEO, greeted, her voice infused with determination and purpose. "Today, we're tackling the important topic of maintaining culture through growth and change. As our organization evolves and expands, it's essential that we preserve the essence of who we are and what we stand for."

David nodded in agreement, his expression reflecting a deep commitment to preserving the cultural identity of the organization amidst change. "Maintaining culture through growth and change requires us to be intentional and proactive in preserving our core values, beliefs, and behaviors."

He clicked the remote, and a slide titled "Maintaining Culture Through Growth and Change" appeared on the screen, outlining key points: Cultural Preservation, Communication, Leadership Alignment, and Adaptability.

"Let's start with cultural preservation," David began. "Preserving our culture means staying true to our core values, beliefs, and identity, even as we grow and evolve as an organization. It means maintaining the same level of integrity, collaboration, and innovation that have defined us from the beginning."

Tom, the HR manager, raised his hand. "How can we ensure that our culture remains intact as we scale and expand?"

"We can prioritize cultural fit in our hiring processes to ensure that new employees share our values and are aligned with our cultural priorities," David suggested. "We can also provide orientation and onboarding programs to introduce new employees to our culture, values, and expectations, and integrate them into our organizational community."

Sarah nodded in agreement. "Communication is another essential aspect of maintaining culture through growth and change. We need to communicate openly and transparently with employees about changes, challenges, and opportunities facing the organization. By keeping employees informed and

CHAPTER 7: DEVELOPING AND SUSTAINING CULTURE

engaged, we build trust and confidence and foster a sense of ownership and commitment to our cultural journey."

Lisa, the marketing director, added, "Leadership alignment is also critical for maintaining culture through growth and change. Our leaders play a key role in setting the tone, modeling behaviors, and reinforcing cultural norms and expectations. By ensuring that our leaders are aligned with our cultural priorities and lead by example, we create a strong foundation for cultural continuity and consistency."

David smiled at her contribution. "Exactly, Lisa. Adaptability is another important aspect of maintaining culture through growth and change. While it's essential to preserve our core values and identity, we also need to be flexible and adaptable to new ideas, perspectives, and ways of working. By embracing change and innovation while staying true to our cultural roots, we can navigate growth and transformation successfully while preserving the essence of who we are as an organization."

He moved on to the next point. "Measuring the impact of our efforts to maintain culture through growth and change is essential for ensuring that we're achieving our desired outcomes and driving meaningful change. We can track key metrics such as employee engagement, satisfaction, and retention to evaluate the effectiveness of our strategies and make adjustments as needed to ensure that our culture remains strong and vibrant amidst change."

Mark, the head of engineering, spoke up. "How can we ensure that our efforts to maintain culture are inclusive and equitable for all employees?"

"We can involve employees in the process and solicit their feedback and ideas for preserving our culture through growth and change," David replied. "This may include conducting surveys, focus groups, or town hall meetings to gather input from employees at all levels of the organization and incorporating their perspectives into our strategies and action plans. By prioritizing inclusivity and equity in our efforts to maintain culture, we ensure that all employees feel valued, respected, and empowered to contribute to our cultural journey."

Sarah stood up, feeling a sense of determination and purpose. "Thank you, David. Maintaining culture through growth and change is essential for preserving the essence of who we are as an organization. Let's commit to staying true to our core values, communicating openly and transparently, aligning our leaders, and embracing change while preserving our cultural identity as we continue to grow and evolve."

With their commitment to maintaining culture through growth and change, the leadership team of Innovatech felt empowered to navigate the challenges and opportunities of organizational expansion and transformation while preserving the essence of their cultural identity. David felt a renewed sense of optimism and purpose for the journey ahead as they continued to prioritize cultural development and sustainability.

Overcoming Resistance to Cultural Change

In the determined atmosphere of Innovatech's meeting room, the leadership team confronted the challenge of overcoming resistance to cultural change within the organization. David Lawson understood that navigating resistance was essential for driving successful cultural transformation and fostering a culture of openness, adaptability, and growth.

"Good morning, everyone," Sarah Mitchell, the CEO, greeted, her voice filled with resolve and determination. "Today, we're tackling the critical topic of overcoming resistance to cultural change. As we strive to evolve and improve our organizational culture, we must anticipate and address the challenges and obstacles that may arise along the way."

David nodded in agreement, his expression reflecting a deep understanding of the complexities of cultural change. "Overcoming resistance to cultural change requires us to approach the process with empathy, patience, and a willingness to listen and learn from others."

He clicked the remote, and a slide titled "Overcoming Resistance to Cultural Change" appeared on the screen, outlining key points: Understanding Resistance, Communication and Engagement, Education and Training, and Leading by Example.

"Let's start with understanding resistance," David began. "Resistance to cultural change can stem from a variety of factors, including fear of the unknown, uncertainty about the future, and attachment to the status quo. By understanding the underlying reasons for resistance, we can address the concerns and motivations of employees more effectively and develop strategies to overcome resistance."

Tom, the HR manager, raised his hand. "How can we effectively communicate and engage with employees to overcome resistance to cultural change?"

"We can communicate openly and transparently with employees about the reasons for the change, the expected benefits, and the role they play in the process," David suggested. "By providing opportunities for dialogue, feedback, and participation, we can engage employees in the change process and build a sense of ownership and commitment to our cultural journey."

Sarah nodded in agreement. "Education and training are also essential for overcoming resistance to cultural change. We need to provide employees with the knowledge, skills, and resources they need to understand the change, adapt to new ways of working, and thrive in our evolving culture. By investing in training programs, workshops, and resources, we can empower employees to embrace change and contribute to our cultural transformation."

Lisa, the marketing director, added, "Leading by example is another powerful way to overcome resistance to cultural change. Our leaders play a key role in shaping the culture of our organization, and their actions and behaviors set the tone for others. By demonstrating a commitment to the change, modeling desired behaviors, and reinforcing cultural norms and expectations, our leaders can inspire and motivate others to embrace the change and contribute to our cultural transformation."

David smiled at her contribution. "Exactly, Lisa. By leading with empathy, authenticity, and humility, our leaders can create a supportive and inclusive environment where employees feel valued, respected, and empowered to embrace change and contribute to our cultural journey."

He moved on to the next point. "Measuring the impact of our efforts to overcome resistance to cultural change is essential for ensuring that we're making progress and achieving our desired outcomes. We can track key metrics such as employee engagement, satisfaction, and performance to evaluate the effectiveness of our strategies and make adjustments as needed to address any lingering resistance."

Mark, the head of engineering, spoke up. "How can we ensure that our efforts to overcome resistance are sustainable and lasting?"

"We can embed change management principles and practices into our organizational processes and systems to ensure that change is managed effectively and sustainably," David replied. "This may include establishing clear goals and objectives, developing action plans and timelines, and providing ongoing support and resources to employees throughout the change process. By fostering a culture of continuous improvement and learning, we can ensure that our efforts to overcome resistance to cultural change are sustainable and lasting."

Sarah stood up, feeling a sense of determination and purpose. "Thank you, David. Overcoming resistance to cultural change is essential for driving our organizational transformation and achieving our goals. Let's commit to approaching the process with empathy, patience, and a willingness to learn as we continue to evolve and improve our organizational culture."

With their commitment to overcoming resistance to cultural change, the leadership team of Innovatech felt empowered to navigate the challenges and complexities of cultural transformation with confidence and determination. David felt a renewed sense of optimism and purpose for the journey ahead as they continued to prioritize cultural development and sustainability.

Continuous Improvement and Cultural Evolution

In the forward-thinking atmosphere of Innovatech's meeting room, the leadership team delved into the concept of continuous improvement and cultural evolution within the organization. David Lawson understood that fostering a culture of continuous learning, adaptation, and innovation was essential for staying agile and competitive in a rapidly changing business landscape.

"Good morning, everyone," Sarah Mitchell, the CEO, greeted, her voice brimming with energy and enthusiasm. "Today, we're exploring the dynamic process of continuous improvement and cultural evolution. As our organization grows and evolves, it's essential that we embrace change and strive for excellence in everything we do."

David nodded in agreement, his expression reflecting a deep commitment to fostering a culture of continuous improvement within the organization. "Continuous improvement and cultural evolution require us to be open to new ideas, feedback, and opportunities for growth. It's about constantly challenging ourselves to do better and be better as individuals and as an organization."

He clicked the remote, and a slide titled "Continuous Improvement and Cultural Evolution" appeared on the screen, outlining key points: Learning from Experience, Feedback Mechanisms, Experimentation and Innovation, and Adaptability.

"Let's start with learning from experience," David began. "Continuous improvement begins with reflection and learning from our successes and failures. By taking the time to analyze our experiences, identify areas for improvement, and apply what we've learned to future endeavors, we can continuously grow and evolve as individuals and as an organization."

Tom, the HR manager, raised his hand. "How can we create feedback mechanisms to facilitate continuous improvement and cultural evolution?"

"We can solicit feedback from employees at all levels of the organization through surveys, focus groups, suggestion boxes, and one-on-one meetings," David suggested. "By providing opportunities for employees to share their ideas, concerns, and suggestions, we can gain valuable insights into our organizational strengths and weaknesses and identify opportunities for improvement."

Sarah nodded in agreement. "Experimentation and innovation are also essential for driving continuous improvement and cultural evolution. We need to encourage employees to think creatively, take calculated risks, and explore new ideas and approaches. By fostering a culture of experimentation and innovation, we can uncover new opportunities for growth and differentiation and stay ahead of the curve in a rapidly changing market."

Lisa, the marketing director, added, "Adaptability is another critical aspect of continuous improvement and cultural evolution. We need to be agile and responsive to changing market conditions, customer needs, and technological advancements. By embracing change and proactively seeking out opportunities for growth and innovation, we can position ourselves for long-term success in an increasingly competitive landscape."

David smiled at her contribution. "Exactly, Lisa. By fostering a culture of continuous improvement and cultural evolution, we create a dynamic and resilient organization that is capable of adapting and thriving in a rapidly changing world."

He moved on to the next point. "Measuring the impact of our efforts to drive continuous improvement and cultural evolution is essential for ensuring that we're making progress and achieving our desired outcomes. We can track key metrics such as employee engagement, satisfaction, and performance to evaluate the effectiveness of our strategies and make adjustments as needed to drive continuous improvement and cultural evolution."

Mark, the head of engineering, spoke up. "How can we ensure that our efforts to drive continuous improvement and cultural evolution are aligned with our organizational goals and objectives?"

"We can align our efforts with our organizational goals and objectives by setting clear priorities, establishing metrics and targets for success, and regularly reviewing and reassessing our progress," David replied. "By aligning our efforts with our organizational goals, we ensure that our initiatives contribute to our overall success and drive meaningful change and improvement."

Sarah stood up, feeling a sense of excitement and purpose. "Thank you, David. Continuous improvement and cultural evolution are essential for driving our organization forward and achieving our goals. Let's commit to embracing change, fostering innovation, and challenging ourselves to do better and be better every day as we continue to evolve and grow as an organization."

With their commitment to continuous improvement and cultural evolution, the leadership team of Innovatech felt empowered to drive positive change and innovation within the organization. David felt a renewed sense of optimism and purpose for the journey ahead as they continued to prioritize learning, adaptation, and growth in shaping the organization's culture.

8

Chapter 8: Measuring and Evaluating Culture

Key Metrics for Assessing Organizational Culture

In the analytical ambiance of Innovatech's meeting room, the leadership team delved into the crucial task of measuring and evaluating organizational culture. David Lawson understood that quantifying culture was essential for understanding its impact on performance, engagement, and success.

"Good morning, everyone," Sarah Mitchell, the CEO, greeted, her voice carrying a tone of purpose and determination. "Today, we're diving into the important topic of measuring and evaluating organizational culture. As we strive to build a culture of excellence and innovation, it's essential that we have the tools and metrics to assess our progress and identify areas for improvement."

David nodded in agreement, his expression reflecting a deep understanding of the importance of data-driven decision-making in shaping organizational culture. "Measuring and evaluating culture allows us to track our progress, identify trends, and make informed decisions about our cultural initiatives."

He clicked the remote, and a slide titled "Key Metrics for Assessing Organizational Culture" appeared on the screen, outlining key points: Employee Engagement, Cultural Alignment, Leadership Effectiveness, and Performance Metrics.

"Let's start with employee engagement," David began. "Employee engagement is a key indicator of organizational culture. Engaged employees are more likely to be committed, productive, and satisfied in their roles, and they play a critical role in driving organizational performance and success. By measuring employee engagement through surveys, feedback mechanisms, and performance evaluations, we can assess the health of our culture and identify opportunities for improvement."

Tom, the HR manager, raised his hand. "How can we ensure that our employee engagement surveys are effective and meaningful?"

"We can design our surveys to capture feedback on key aspects of organizational culture, such as leadership effectiveness, communication, teamwork, and recognition," David suggested. "We can also ensure that our surveys are anonymous, confidential, and inclusive to encourage honest and candid feedback from employees at all levels of the organization. By soliciting input from employees on their perceptions and experiences, we gain valuable insights into the strengths and weaknesses of our culture and can take action to address any issues or concerns."

Sarah nodded in agreement. "Cultural alignment is another important metric for assessing organizational culture. Cultural alignment refers to the extent to which our employees' beliefs, values, and behaviors are aligned with our organizational values, mission, and goals. By measuring cultural alignment through surveys, assessments, and interviews, we can gauge the degree to which our culture is resonating with our employees and driving desired behaviors and outcomes."

Lisa, the marketing director, added, "Leadership effectiveness is also crucial for assessing organizational culture. Our leaders play a key role in shaping the culture of our organization and setting the tone for others. By measuring leadership effectiveness through 360-degree feedback, performance evaluations, and other assessments, we can identify areas for improvement and provide targeted development opportunities for our leaders."

David smiled at her contribution. "Exactly, Lisa. Performance metrics are another valuable tool for assessing organizational culture. Performance metrics, such as productivity, profitability, customer satisfaction, and employee turnover, provide tangible indicators of the impact of culture on organizational outcomes. By tracking performance metrics over time and comparing them to industry benchmarks and organizational goals, we can assess the effectiveness of our cultural initiatives and make data-driven decisions to drive continuous improvement and innovation."

He moved on to the next point. "Measuring and evaluating culture requires us to be strategic and intentional in selecting the right metrics and tools for assessing our progress and identifying areas for improvement. By leveraging a combination of quantitative and qualitative data, we can gain a comprehensive understanding of our organizational culture and take action to shape it in alignment with our values, mission, and goals."

Mark, the head of engineering, spoke up. "How can we ensure that our efforts to measure and evaluate culture are integrated into our day-to-day operations and decision-making processes?"

"We can embed culture metrics into our performance management systems, employee feedback processes, and leadership development programs to ensure that they are integrated into our organizational practices and norms," David replied. "By making culture measurement and evaluation a priority in our day-to-day operations, we create a culture of accountability, transparency, and continuous improvement where everyone is empowered to contribute to our cultural journey."

Sarah stood up, feeling a sense of satisfaction and purpose. "Thank you, David. Measuring and evaluating culture is essential for driving our organizational transformation and achieving our goals. Let's commit to leveraging data and insights to assess our progress, identify opportunities for improvement, and shape our culture in alignment with our values, mission, and goals."

With their commitment to measuring and evaluating culture, the leadership team of Innovatech felt empowered to drive positive change and innovation within the organization. David felt a renewed sense of optimism and purpose for the journey ahead as they continued to prioritize data-driven decision-making and cultural development in shaping the organization's future.

CHAPTER 8: MEASURING AND EVALUATING CULTURE

Tools and Techniques for Culture Assessment

In the methodical atmosphere of Innovatech's meeting room, the leadership team delved into the practical aspect of assessing organizational culture. David Lawson understood that selecting the right tools and techniques was essential for obtaining accurate insights into the organization's cultural dynamics.

"Good morning, everyone," Sarah Mitchell, the CEO, greeted, her voice resonating with purpose and determination. "Today, we're exploring the tools and techniques for culture assessment. As we strive to understand and improve our organizational culture, it's crucial that we choose the most effective methods for gathering data and insights."

David nodded in agreement, his expression reflecting a deep understanding of the significance of selecting appropriate tools for culture assessment. "Using the right tools and techniques allows us to gather reliable data and gain meaningful insights into our organizational culture, enabling us to make informed decisions and drive positive change."

He clicked the remote, and a slide titled "Tools and Techniques for Culture Assessment" appeared on the screen, outlining key points: Surveys, Interviews and Focus Groups, Observation, and Cultural Audits.

"Let's start with surveys," David began. "Surveys are a widely used tool for culture assessment, as they provide a systematic way to collect quantitative data on employees' perceptions, attitudes, and experiences. By designing surveys that target specific aspects of organizational culture, such as leadership effectiveness, communication, and teamwork, we can gather valuable insights into the strengths and weaknesses of our culture and identify opportunities for improvement."

Tom, the HR manager, raised his hand. "How can we ensure that our surveys are effective and yield meaningful results?"

"We can design our surveys to be clear, concise, and focused on relevant aspects of organizational culture," David suggested. "We can also ensure that our surveys are anonymous, confidential, and inclusive to encourage honest and candid feedback from employees at all levels of the organization. By soliciting input from a diverse range of employees, we can gain a comprehensive understanding of our organizational culture and identify areas for improvement."

Sarah nodded in agreement. "Interviews and focus groups are another valuable tool for culture assessment. By conducting one-on-one interviews or group discussions with employees, we can gather qualitative data on their perceptions, experiences, and perspectives on organizational culture. These insights can complement the findings from surveys and provide a deeper understanding of the underlying dynamics of our culture."

Lisa, the marketing director, added, "Observation is also a powerful technique for culture assessment. By observing employee interactions, behaviors, and practices in the workplace, we can gain firsthand insights into the informal norms, rituals, and values that shape our organizational culture. This can help us identify areas of alignment and misalignment between our espoused values and our actual behaviors."

David smiled at her contribution. "Exactly, Lisa. Cultural audits are another valuable tool for culture assessment. Cultural audits involve systematically reviewing and analyzing various aspects of organizational culture, such as policies, practices, and artifacts, to assess their alignment with our values, mission, and goals. By conducting cultural audits regularly, we can track our progress, identify areas for improvement, and ensure that our cultural initiatives are driving meaningful change and improvement."

He moved on to the next point. "Selecting the right tools and techniques for culture assessment requires us to be strategic and intentional in our approach. By leveraging a combination of quantitative and qualitative methods, we can gain a comprehensive understanding of our organizational culture and identify opportunities for improvement. Ultimately, our goal is to use data and insights to inform our decision-making and drive positive change within the organization."

Mark, the head of engineering, spoke up. "How can we ensure that our culture assessment efforts are integrated into our broader organizational strategy and goals?"

"We can align our culture assessment efforts with our organizational strategy and goals by setting clear objectives, establishing metrics and targets for success, and regularly reviewing and reassessing our progress," David replied. "By integrating culture assessment into our broader organizational practices and processes, we ensure that it becomes an ongoing and integral part of how we operate and make decisions."

Sarah stood up, feeling a sense of satisfaction and purpose. "Thank you, David. Selecting the right tools and techniques for culture assessment is essential for driving our organizational transformation and achieving our goals. Let's commit to leveraging data and insights to assess our culture effectively and drive positive change within the organization."

With their commitment to using the right tools and techniques for culture assessment, the leadership team of Innovatech felt empowered to gain meaningful insights into their organizational culture and drive positive change and innovation. David felt a renewed sense of optimism and purpose for the journey ahead as they continued to prioritize data-driven decision-making and cultural development in shaping the organization's future.

Analyzing and Interpreting Culture Data

In the analytical ambiance of Innovatech's meeting room, the leadership team delved into the intricate process of analyzing and interpreting culture data. David Lawson understood that making sense of the gathered data was essential for deriving actionable insights and driving meaningful change within the organization.

"Good morning, everyone," Sarah Mitchell, the CEO, greeted, her voice infused with determination and focus. "Today, we're delving into the critical task of analyzing and interpreting culture data. As we strive to understand our organizational culture better, it's essential that we uncover meaningful insights that can guide our decision-making and drive positive change."

David nodded in agreement, his expression reflecting a deep understanding of the importance of data analysis in shaping organizational culture. "Analyzing and interpreting culture data allows us to identify trends, patterns, and areas for improvement, enabling us to make informed decisions and take targeted actions to strengthen our culture."

He clicked the remote, and a slide titled "Analyzing and Interpreting Culture Data" appeared on the screen, outlining key points: Data Review, Theme Identification, Root Cause Analysis, and Action Planning.

"Let's start with data review," David began. "Data review

involves systematically reviewing and organizing the data collected from surveys, interviews, observations, and cultural audits. By aggregating and summarizing the data, we can gain a holistic understanding of our organizational culture and identify key themes and trends that require further exploration."

Tom, the HR manager, raised his hand. "How can we ensure that our data review process is thorough and comprehensive?"

"We can use data visualization tools and techniques to organize and present the data in a clear and meaningful way," David suggested. "By creating charts, graphs, and dashboards, we can visualize trends, patterns, and relationships in the data, making it easier to identify key insights and areas for further analysis."

Sarah nodded in agreement. "Theme identification is another important step in analyzing culture data. By identifying common themes and patterns across the data, we can uncover underlying issues, challenges, and opportunities within our organizational culture. This can help us prioritize areas for improvement and develop targeted strategies and action plans to address them."

Lisa, the marketing director, added, "Root cause analysis is also crucial for interpreting culture data. By drilling down into the underlying causes of identified issues and challenges, we can uncover the root causes that are driving them. This can help us develop more effective solutions and interventions that target the underlying drivers of cultural dynamics."

David smiled at her contribution. "Exactly, Lisa. Action planning is the final step in analyzing and interpreting culture data. By translating our insights into actionable strategies and initiatives, we can drive meaningful change and improvement within the organization. This may involve developing targeted interventions, implementing new policies or programs, or providing additional training and support to employees."

He moved on to the next point. "Analyzing and interpreting culture data requires us to be strategic and intentional in our approach. By leveraging a combination of quantitative and qualitative methods, we can gain a comprehensive understanding of our organizational culture and identify opportunities for improvement. Ultimately, our goal is to use data and insights to inform our decision-making and drive positive change within the organization."

Mark, the head of engineering, spoke up. "How can we ensure that our analysis and interpretation of culture data are aligned with our organizational strategy and goals?"

"We can align our analysis and interpretation of culture data with our organizational strategy and goals by focusing on key priorities and objectives," David replied. "By linking our insights to our broader organizational goals, we ensure that our efforts to drive cultural change are aligned with our strategic direction and contribute to our overall success."

Sarah stood up, feeling a sense of satisfaction and purpose. "Thank you, David. Analyzing and interpreting culture data is essential for driving our organizational transformation and achieving our goals. Let's commit to leveraging data and insights to assess our culture effectively and drive positive change within the organization."

With their commitment to analyzing and interpreting culture data, the leadership team of Innovatech felt empowered to gain meaningful insights into their organizational culture and drive positive change and innovation. David felt a renewed sense of optimism and purpose for the journey ahead as they continued to prioritize data-driven decision-making and cultural development in shaping the organization's future.

Reporting and Sharing Culture Metrics

In the collaborative setting of Innovatech's meeting room, the leadership team delved into the crucial task of reporting and sharing culture metrics. David Lawson understood that effectively communicating culture data was essential for fostering transparency, accountability, and alignment within the organization.

"Good morning, everyone," Sarah Mitchell, the CEO, greeted, her voice filled with energy and purpose. "Today, we're focusing on the important task of reporting and sharing culture metrics. As we strive to build a culture of openness and accountability, it's essential that we share our findings and insights with transparency and clarity."

David nodded in agreement, his expression reflecting a deep understanding of the importance of communication in shaping organizational culture. "Reporting and sharing culture metrics allows us to keep stakeholders informed, engaged, and aligned with our cultural initiatives, enabling us to drive positive change and improvement within the organization."

He clicked the remote, and a slide titled "Reporting and Sharing Culture Metrics" appeared on the screen, outlining key points: Audience Identification, Report Design, Communication Channels, and Action Planning.

"Let's start with audience identification," David began. "Identifying our target audience is essential for tailoring our reporting and communication efforts to their needs and preferences. Our audience may include employees at all levels of the organization, as well as external stakeholders such as customers, investors, and partners. By understanding their interests, concerns, and information needs, we can ensure that our reporting efforts are relevant, meaningful, and impactful."

Tom, the HR manager, raised his hand. "How can we ensure that our reports are designed effectively and engagingly?"

"We can design our reports to be clear, concise, and visually appealing," David suggested. "By using charts, graphs, and other visual aids, we can present our findings in a way that is easy to understand and digest. We can also include narrative summaries and key takeaways to highlight the most important insights and recommendations."

Sarah nodded in agreement. "Communication channels are another important consideration in reporting and sharing culture metrics. We need to use a variety of channels and platforms to reach our target audience effectively, such as email, intranet, social media, and town hall meetings. By leveraging multiple channels, we can ensure that our messages reach employees wherever they are and in a format that resonates with them."

Lisa, the marketing director, added, "Action planning is also crucial for reporting and sharing culture metrics. By translating our findings and insights into actionable strategies and initiatives, we can drive meaningful change and improvement within the organization. This may involve developing targeted interventions, implementing new policies or programs, or providing additional training and support to employees."

David smiled at her contribution. "Exactly, Lisa. By sharing our culture metrics with transparency and clarity, we foster a culture of openness, accountability, and continuous improvement within the organization. This creates a sense of ownership and commitment among employees, empowering them to contribute to our cultural journey and drive positive change and innovation."

He moved on to the next point. "Reporting and sharing culture metrics requires us to be strategic and intentional in our approach. By tailoring our efforts to the needs and preferences of our target audience, we ensure that our messages are relevant, meaningful, and impactful. Ultimately, our goal is to use communication as a powerful tool for driving cultural change and improvement within the organization."

Mark, the head of engineering, spoke up. "How can we ensure that our reporting and sharing efforts are aligned with our broader organizational strategy and goals?"

"We can align our reporting and sharing efforts with our organizational strategy and goals by focusing on key priorities and objectives," David replied. "By linking our communication efforts to our broader organizational goals, we ensure that our messages are relevant and impactful. This creates a sense of purpose and direction among employees, motivating them to contribute to our cultural journey and drive positive change within the organization."

Sarah stood up, feeling a sense of satisfaction and purpose. "Thank you, David. Reporting and sharing culture metrics is essential for driving our organizational transformation and achieving our goals. Let's commit to leveraging communication as a powerful tool for fostering transparency, accountability, and alignment within the organization."

With their commitment to reporting and sharing culture metrics, the leadership team of Innovatech felt empowered to keep stakeholders informed, engaged, and aligned with their cultural initiatives. David felt a renewed sense of optimism and purpose for the journey ahead as they continued to prioritize communication and transparency in shaping the organization's future.

Using Feedback for Cultural Enhancement

In the collaborative setting of Innovatech's meeting room, the leadership team focused on the crucial task of using feedback for cultural enhancement. David Lawson understood that leveraging feedback was essential for fostering continuous improvement and driving positive change within the organization.

"Good morning, everyone," Sarah Mitchell, the CEO, greeted, her voice brimming with enthusiasm and determination. "Today, we're diving into the important topic of using feedback for cultural enhancement. As we strive to build a culture of openness and collaboration, it's essential that we actively seek and respond to feedback from our stakeholders."

David nodded in agreement, his expression reflecting a deep understanding of the importance of feedback in shaping organizational culture. "Using feedback for cultural enhancement allows us to identify areas for improvement, address issues and concerns, and reinforce positive behaviors and practices within the organization."

He clicked the remote, and a slide titled "Using Feedback for Cultural Enhancement" appeared on the screen, outlining key points: Feedback Collection, Analysis and Action, Feedback Loops, and Continuous Improvement.

"Let's start with feedback collection," David began. "Collecting feedback from employees, customers, and other stakeholders is essential for gaining insights into their perceptions, experiences, and expectations regarding our organizational

CHAPTER 8: MEASURING AND EVALUATING CULTURE

culture. We can use a variety of methods to collect feedback, such as surveys, focus groups, suggestion boxes, and one-on-one meetings, to ensure that we capture diverse perspectives and opinions."

Tom, the HR manager, raised his hand. "How can we ensure that our feedback collection efforts are effective and meaningful?"

"We can design our feedback collection processes to be transparent, inclusive, and responsive to the needs and preferences of our stakeholders," David suggested. "By clearly communicating the purpose of our feedback collection efforts, ensuring anonymity and confidentiality where appropriate, and providing opportunities for follow-up and dialogue, we can encourage honest and candid feedback from our stakeholders."

Sarah nodded in agreement. "Analysis and action are another important aspect of using feedback for cultural enhancement. Once we've collected feedback, we need to analyze it to identify key themes, trends, and areas for improvement. We can then develop targeted action plans and initiatives to address the issues and concerns raised by our stakeholders and reinforce positive behaviors and practices within the organization."

Lisa, the marketing director, added, "Feedback loops are also crucial for using feedback for cultural enhancement. By closing the loop with our stakeholders and communicating the outcomes of our feedback collection efforts, we demonstrate that we value their input and are committed to addressing their concerns. This fosters trust, engagement, and accountability within the organization."

David smiled at her contribution. "Exactly, Lisa. By closing the feedback loop with our stakeholders, we create a culture of openness, transparency, and continuous improvement within the organization. This enables us to build trust, strengthen relationships, and drive positive change and innovation."

He moved on to the next point. "Using feedback for cultural enhancement requires us to be proactive and responsive in our approach. By actively seeking and responding to feedback from our stakeholders, we demonstrate our commitment to listening, learning, and evolving as an organization. Ultimately, our goal is to use feedback as a catalyst for cultural enhancement and organizational improvement."

Mark, the head of engineering, spoke up. "How can we ensure that our feedback collection and action efforts are aligned with our broader organizational strategy and goals?"

"We can align our feedback collection and action efforts with our organizational strategy and goals by focusing on key priorities and objectives," David replied. "By linking our feedback initiatives to our broader organizational goals, we ensure that our efforts contribute to our overall success and drive meaningful change and improvement within the organization."

Sarah stood up, feeling a sense of satisfaction and purpose. "Thank you, David. Using feedback for cultural enhancement is essential for driving our organizational transformation and achieving our goals. Let's commit to actively seeking and responding to feedback from our stakeholders and using it as a catalyst for continuous improvement and innovation within the organization."

With their commitment to using feedback for cultural enhancement, the leadership team of Innovatech felt empowered to build a culture of openness, collaboration, and continuous improvement. David felt a renewed sense of optimism and purpose for the journey ahead as they continued to prioritize feedback and stakeholder engagement in shaping the organization's future.

Chapter 9: The Impact of Technology on Culture

Technology as a Cultural Enabler

In the modern conference room of Innovatech, the leadership team gathered to explore the profound impact of technology on organizational culture. David Lawson, the Chief Technology Officer, understood that technology served as more than just a tool; it was a catalyst for cultural transformation.

"Good morning, everyone," Sarah Mitchell, the CEO, greeted, her voice resonating with anticipation. "Today, we're delving into the fascinating topic of the impact of technology on organizational culture. As we navigate the digital age, it's crucial to understand how technology shapes our values, behaviors, and interactions within the organization."

David nodded, his eyes gleaming with enthusiasm. "Technology has become an integral part of our daily lives, both inside and outside the workplace. It not only facilitates our tasks but also influences the way we communicate, collaborate, and innovate."

He clicked the remote, and a slide titled "Technology as a Cultural Enabler" appeared on the screen, depicting images of smartphones, laptops, and digital collaboration tools.

"Let's start with technology as a cultural enabler," David began. "Technology has the power to break down barriers and bring people together, regardless of geographical locations or organizational hierarchies. With tools like video conferencing, instant messaging, and collaborative platforms, we can foster a culture of openness, transparency, and collaboration within the organization."

Tom, the HR manager, raised his hand. "How does technology enable cultural diversity and inclusion?"

"Technology provides us with the opportunity to create inclusive spaces where diverse voices are heard and valued," David explained. "Through virtual meetings and online forums, employees from different backgrounds and locations can contribute ideas, share perspectives, and collaborate on projects in real-time. This promotes diversity of thought and fosters a culture of inclusion and belonging."

Sarah nodded in agreement. "Technology also enables flexibility and agility within the organization. With remote work tools and mobile applications, employees can work from anywhere, at any time, allowing for greater work-life balance and autonomy. This flexibility enhances employee satisfaction and engagement, ultimately contributing to a positive organizational culture."

Lisa, the marketing director, added, "Technology accelerates innovation and creativity by providing access to information, resources, and tools. With digital platforms for brainstorming, prototyping, and sharing ideas, employees can collaborate more effectively and bring new products and solutions to market faster. This culture of innovation drives competitiveness and growth within the organization."

David smiled at her contribution. "Exactly, Lisa. Technology serves as a catalyst for cultural change and transformation, enabling us to adapt to the evolving needs and expectations of our employees and customers. By embracing technology as a cultural enabler, we can create a dynamic and forward-thinking organization that thrives in the digital age."

He moved on to the next point. "Embracing technology as a cultural enabler requires us to be proactive and strategic in our approach. By leveraging the latest tools and technologies, we can foster a culture of innovation, collaboration, and inclusion that drives organizational success and growth."

Mark, the head of engineering, spoke up. "How can we ensure that our use of technology aligns with our organizational values and goals?"

"We can align our use of technology with our organizational values and goals by integrating technology into our cultural initiatives and practices," David replied. "By incorporating technology into our communication, collaboration, and learning strategies, we ensure that it supports and enhances our cultural objectives. This creates a harmonious relationship between technology and culture, driving positive outcomes for the organization as a whole."

Sarah stood up, feeling a sense of excitement and possibility. "Thank you, David. Technology is indeed a powerful enabler of cultural change and transformation. Let's commit to embracing technology in a way that fosters innovation, collaboration, and inclusion within the organization."

With their commitment to leveraging technology as a cultural enabler, the leadership team of Innovatech felt empowered to navigate the complexities of the digital age and drive positive change within the organization. David felt a renewed sense of purpose and excitement as they embarked on this journey of cultural transformation in the digital era.

Digital Transformation and Culture

In the sleek conference room of Innovatech, the leadership team continued their exploration of technology's influence on organizational culture. David Lawson, the Chief Technology Officer, knew that digital transformation was not just about adopting new tools; it was about fundamentally reshaping the way people worked and interacted within the organization.

"Good morning, everyone," Sarah Mitchell, the CEO, greeted, her voice filled with anticipation. "Today, we're delving deeper into the impact of technology on organizational culture, specifically focusing on digital transformation. As we embrace new technologies and ways of working, it's essential to understand how they shape our culture and mindset."

David nodded, his gaze focused on the screen displaying images of automation, artificial intelligence, and data analytics. "Digital transformation is revolutionizing the way we do business, from streamlining processes to enhancing customer experiences. But it's also transforming our culture, influencing how we collaborate, innovate, and adapt to change."

He clicked the remote, and a slide titled "Digital Transformation and Culture" appeared on the screen, depicting a journey from traditional to digital processes.

"Let's start with the impact of digital transformation on

workplace culture," David began. "As we automate routine tasks and embrace data-driven decision-making, employees are empowered to focus on more strategic and creative endeavors. This shift from manual to digital processes fosters a culture of innovation and agility, where experimentation and risk-taking are encouraged."

Tom, the HR manager, raised his hand. "How does digital transformation affect leadership and management?"

"Digital transformation requires leaders to adopt new mindsets and skill sets," David explained. "Leaders must embrace change, inspire collaboration, and leverage data to drive informed decisions. By leading by example and championing digital initiatives, they set the tone for a culture that embraces innovation and continuous improvement."

Sarah nodded in agreement. "Digital transformation also promotes transparency and accountability within the organization. With digital tools for tracking performance and sharing information, employees have access to real-time data and insights, empowering them to make informed decisions and take ownership of their work. This culture of transparency fosters trust and collaboration among teams."

Lisa, the marketing director, added, "Digital transformation enhances employee engagement and satisfaction by providing opportunities for skill development and career advancement. With online learning platforms and digital performance management systems, employees can access training and development resources tailored to their needs and aspirations. This investment in employee growth reinforces a culture of learning and development."

David smiled at her contribution. "Exactly, Lisa. Digital transformation is not just about adopting new technologies; it's about creating a culture that embraces change and innovation. By empowering employees with the tools and resources they need to succeed in the digital age, we foster a culture of agility, collaboration, and continuous improvement that drives organizational success."

He moved on to the next point. "Embracing digital transformation requires us to be proactive and adaptive in our approach. By embracing new technologies and ways of working, we can create a culture that thrives in the digital age and drives innovation and growth."

Mark, the head of engineering, spoke up. "How can we ensure that our digital transformation efforts are aligned with our organizational values and goals?"

"We can align our digital transformation efforts with our organizational values and goals by integrating digital initiatives into our cultural practices and processes," David replied. "By leveraging technology to support our cultural objectives, we ensure that our digital transformation efforts contribute to our overall success and drive positive outcomes for the organization as a whole."

Sarah stood up, feeling a sense of excitement and possibility. "Thank you, David. Digital transformation has the power to revolutionize our culture and mindset. Let's commit to embracing this transformation in a way that fosters innovation, collaboration, and growth within the organization."

With their commitment to embracing digital transformation, the leadership team of Innovatech felt empowered to navigate the complexities of the digital age and drive positive change within the organization. David felt a renewed sense of purpose and excitement as they embarked on this journey of cultural transformation in the digital era.

Leveraging Social Media for Cultural Development

In the dynamic conference room of Innovatech, the leadership team delved deeper into the exploration of technology's influence on organizational culture. David Lawson, the Chief Technology Officer, understood that social media was more than just a platform for communication; it was a powerful tool for shaping organizational identity and fostering a sense of community.

"Good morning, everyone," Sarah Mitchell, the CEO, greeted, her voice filled with enthusiasm. "Today, we're continuing our discussion on the impact of technology on organizational culture, with a focus on leveraging social media for cultural development. As we embrace digital communication channels, it's essential to understand how they can enhance our cultural initiatives and strengthen employee engagement."

David nodded, his eyes scanning the room, filled with anticipation for the discussion ahead. "Social media has transformed the way we connect and communicate, both internally and externally. By leveraging social media platforms, we can amplify our cultural messages, celebrate achievements, and foster meaningful interactions among employees."

He clicked the remote, and a slide titled "Leveraging Social Media for Cultural Development" appeared on the screen, showcasing images of various social media platforms.

"Let's start with the role of social media in internal communication," David began. "Social media platforms such as Yammer, Slack, and Workplace by Facebook provide us with the opportunity to create online communities where employees can share ideas, collaborate on projects, and celebrate successes in real-time. This fosters a sense of belonging and camaraderie

CHAPTER 9: THE IMPACT OF TECHNOLOGY ON CULTURE

among team members, regardless of their physical location."

Tom, the HR manager, raised his hand. "How can we ensure that our use of social media aligns with our cultural values and goals?"

"We can align our social media efforts with our cultural values and goals by establishing clear guidelines and protocols for usage," David explained. "By defining the purpose of each platform, setting expectations for appropriate behavior, and providing training and support to employees, we can ensure that our use of social media reinforces our cultural objectives and contributes to a positive work environment."

Sarah nodded in agreement. "Social media also allows us to showcase our organizational culture to the outside world. By sharing stories, photos, and videos that highlight our values, mission, and employee experiences, we can attract top talent, engage customers, and build our brand reputation as an employer of choice. This external visibility reinforces our cultural identity and strengthens our relationships with stakeholders."

Lisa, the marketing director, added, "Social media enables us to gather feedback and insights from employees in real-time. By monitoring conversations, comments, and engagement metrics, we can identify areas for improvement, address concerns, and celebrate achievements. This two-way dialogue fosters transparency, trust, and collaboration within the organization."

David smiled at her contribution. "Exactly, Lisa. Social media is a powerful tool for cultural development, enabling us to engage employees, showcase our culture, and gather feedback in real-time. By leveraging social media strategically, we can create a dynamic and inclusive culture that drives organizational success."

He moved on to the next point. "Leveraging social media for cultural development requires us to be proactive and strategic in our approach. By defining clear objectives, establishing guidelines for usage, and measuring our impact, we can ensure that our social media efforts contribute to our overall cultural goals and objectives."

Mark, the head of engineering, spoke up. "How can we encourage active participation and engagement on social media platforms?"

"We can encourage participation and engagement on social media platforms by providing opportunities for employees to share their stories, ideas, and experiences," David replied. "By creating a culture of empowerment and recognition, we can motivate employees to contribute to the conversation and become ambassadors for our brand and culture. This grassroots approach fosters a sense of ownership and belonging among employees, driving active participation and engagement on social media."

Sarah stood up, feeling a sense of excitement and possibility. "Thank you, David. Social media has the power to amplify our cultural messages and strengthen employee engagement. Let's commit to leveraging this powerful tool in a way that fosters connection, collaboration, and innovation within the organization."

With their commitment to leveraging social media for cultural development, the leadership team of Innovatech felt empowered to harness the full potential of digital communication channels and drive positive change within the organization. David felt a renewed sense of purpose and excitement as they continued to explore new ways to enhance organizational culture in the digital age.

Remote Work and Virtual Teams

In the technologically advanced conference room of Innovatech, the leadership team delved deeper into the examination of technology's influence on organizational culture. David Lawson, the Chief Technology Officer, understood that remote work and virtual teams were reshaping the traditional dynamics of workplace culture.

"Good morning, everyone," Sarah Mitchell, the CEO, greeted, her voice resonating with purpose. "Today, we're delving into the impact of remote work and virtual teams on organizational culture. As we embrace new ways of working, it's crucial to understand how they shape our cultural norms, values, and interactions."

David nodded, his expression reflecting a deep understanding of the transformative power of remote work. "Remote work and virtual teams have become increasingly prevalent in today's digital age, enabling us to transcend geographical boundaries and tap into global talent pools. But they also present unique challenges and opportunities for shaping organizational culture."

He clicked the remote, and a slide titled "Remote Work and Virtual Teams" appeared on the screen, displaying images of people working from home and virtual team meetings.

"Let's start with the impact of remote work on workplace culture," David began. "Remote work allows employees to have greater flexibility and autonomy in how, when, and where they work. This flexibility fosters a culture of trust, empowerment, and work-life balance, where employees are judged by their results rather than their physical presence."

Tom, the HR manager, raised his hand. "How can we ensure

that remote work aligns with our cultural values and goals?"

"We can align remote work with our cultural values and goals by establishing clear expectations, communication channels, and performance metrics," David explained. "By fostering open communication, providing resources and support, and promoting collaboration among remote teams, we can ensure that remote work enhances our cultural objectives rather than detracting from them."

Sarah nodded in agreement. "Remote work also promotes inclusivity and diversity within the organization. By removing geographical barriers and accommodating different work styles and preferences, remote work enables us to tap into a more diverse talent pool and create a culture that values and celebrates differences."

Lisa, the marketing director, added, "Virtual teams enable us to bring together diverse perspectives and expertise from around the world. By leveraging digital collaboration tools and platforms, virtual teams can collaborate seamlessly on projects, share knowledge and best practices, and drive innovation and creativity within the organization."

David smiled at her contribution. "Exactly, Lisa. Remote work and virtual teams are reshaping the traditional dynamics of workplace culture, enabling us to create a more inclusive, flexible, and collaborative environment. By embracing these new ways of working, we can foster a culture that thrives in the digital age and drives organizational success."

He moved on to the next point. "However, remote work also presents unique challenges, such as maintaining communication, building trust, and fostering a sense of belonging among remote employees. It's essential to address these challenges proactively and implement strategies and practices that support remote work while preserving our cultural values and goals."

Mark, the head of engineering, spoke up. "How can we ensure that remote teams feel connected and engaged with the organization?"

"We can ensure that remote teams feel connected and engaged by providing opportunities for virtual team building, recognition, and socialization," David replied. "By organizing virtual team events, celebrating achievements, and fostering a culture of appreciation and recognition, we can create a sense of belonging and community among remote employees. This strengthens their connection to the organization and reinforces our cultural identity."

Sarah stood up, feeling a sense of determination and optimism. "Thank you, David. Remote work and virtual teams have the potential to transform our organizational culture and drive innovation and collaboration. Let's commit to embracing these new ways of working in a way that fosters inclusivity, flexibility, and connection within the organization."

With their commitment to embracing remote work and virtual teams, the leadership team of Innovatech felt empowered to navigate the challenges and opportunities of the digital age and drive positive change within the organization. David felt a renewed sense of purpose and excitement as they continued to explore new ways to enhance organizational culture in the era of remote work and virtual collaboration.

Cybersecurity and Cultural Considerations

In the high-tech conference room of Innovatech, the leadership team continued their exploration of technology's influence on organizational culture. David Lawson, the Chief Technology Officer, understood that cybersecurity was not just a technical issue; it also had profound cultural implications for the organization.

"Good morning, everyone," Sarah Mitchell, the CEO, greeted, her voice tinged with seriousness. "Today, we're delving into the critical topic of cybersecurity and its cultural considerations. As we embrace digital transformation, it's essential to understand how cybersecurity practices and attitudes shape our organizational culture."

David nodded, his expression grave as he emphasized the importance of cybersecurity in the digital age. "Cybersecurity is not just about protecting our data and systems; it's also about fostering a culture of security awareness, responsibility, and resilience within the organization."

He clicked the remote, and a slide titled "Cybersecurity and Cultural Considerations" appeared on the screen, displaying images of security protocols and awareness training.

"Let's start with the impact of cybersecurity on workplace culture," David began. "Cybersecurity practices and attitudes can significantly influence employee behaviors, attitudes, and perceptions of risk. By promoting a culture of security awareness and accountability, we can empower employees to recognize and mitigate security threats, reducing the risk of data breaches and cyberattacks."

Tom, the HR manager, raised his hand. "How can we ensure that cybersecurity aligns with our cultural values and goals?"

CHAPTER 9: THE IMPACT OF TECHNOLOGY ON CULTURE

"We can ensure that cybersecurity aligns with our cultural values and goals by integrating security awareness and training into our cultural initiatives and practices," David explained. "By providing regular training and resources, promoting a culture of openness and transparency around security incidents, and rewarding positive security behaviors, we can create a culture that values and prioritizes cybersecurity."

Sarah nodded in agreement. "Cybersecurity also plays a critical role in building trust and confidence among customers, partners, and stakeholders. By demonstrating our commitment to protecting their data and privacy, we strengthen our relationships and reputation as a trustworthy and reliable organization."

Lisa, the marketing director, added, "Cybersecurity is everyone's responsibility, from the CEO to the entry-level employee. By fostering a culture of collective responsibility and accountability, we can create a strong defense against cyber threats and vulnerabilities."

David smiled at her contribution. "Exactly, Lisa. Cybersecurity is not just a technical issue; it's a cultural imperative. By embedding security awareness and practices into our organizational culture, we can protect our data, systems, and reputation from cyber threats and vulnerabilities."

He moved on to the next point. "However, fostering a culture of cybersecurity requires more than just technical solutions; it requires a fundamental shift in attitudes, behaviors, and organizational norms. It's essential to cultivate a culture where security is everyone's responsibility and to provide the necessary training and support to empower employees to protect themselves and the organization from cyber threats."

Mark, the head of engineering, spoke up. "How can we

ensure that cybersecurity is a priority for all employees, regardless of their role or department?"

"We can ensure that cybersecurity is a priority for all employees by integrating security awareness and training into our onboarding processes, performance evaluations, and organizational communications," David replied. "By promoting a culture of security from day one and providing ongoing support and resources, we can create a workforce that is knowledgeable, vigilant, and proactive in protecting our organization from cyber threats."

Sarah stood up, feeling a sense of determination and resolve. "Thank you, David. Cybersecurity is indeed a critical aspect of our organizational culture. Let's commit to fostering a culture of security awareness, responsibility, and resilience within the organization, to protect our data, systems, and reputation from cyber threats."

With their commitment to cybersecurity and cultural considerations, the leadership team of Innovatech felt empowered to navigate the challenges of the digital age and drive positive change within the organization. David felt a renewed sense of purpose and determination as they continued to prioritize cybersecurity and build a culture of security awareness and resilience.

Future Trends in Technology and Culture

In the futuristic conference room of Innovatech, the leadership team embarked on a forward-thinking discussion about the intersection of technology and culture. David Lawson, the Chief Technology Officer, understood that anticipating future trends was essential for staying ahead in the rapidly evolving

CHAPTER 9: THE IMPACT OF TECHNOLOGY ON CULTURE

digital landscape.

"Good morning, everyone," Sarah Mitchell, the CEO, greeted, her voice filled with anticipation. "Today, we're exploring future trends in technology and their implications for organizational culture. As we look ahead, it's crucial to understand how emerging technologies will shape the way we work, communicate, and collaborate."

David nodded, his eyes gleaming with excitement for the possibilities ahead. "The pace of technological innovation is accelerating, from artificial intelligence and machine learning to augmented reality and the Internet of Things. These technologies have the potential to revolutionize our organizational culture and redefine the way we interact and engage with each other."

He clicked the remote, and a slide titled "Future Trends in Technology and Culture" appeared on the screen, displaying images of futuristic gadgets and devices.

"Let's start with the impact of artificial intelligence and automation on workplace culture," David began. "As AI and automation become more prevalent in the workplace, they will augment human capabilities, streamline processes, and free up time for more strategic and creative endeavors. This shift will foster a culture of innovation and agility, where employees are empowered to focus on high-value tasks and projects."

Tom, the HR manager, raised his hand. "How can we ensure that AI and automation align with our cultural values and goals?"

"We can ensure that AI and automation align with our cultural values and goals by prioritizing ethical considerations, transparency, and inclusivity in their development and deployment," David explained. "By promoting a culture of responsible AI and automation, we can mitigate risks such as job displacement and algorithmic bias, and ensure that these technologies contribute to our organizational objectives in a positive and ethical manner."

Sarah nodded in agreement. "Emerging technologies such as augmented reality and virtual reality also hold tremendous potential for transforming the way we collaborate and learn within the organization. By creating immersive and interactive experiences, we can break down geographical barriers and foster a culture of creativity and innovation."

Lisa, the marketing director, added, "The Internet of Things is another trend that will revolutionize our organizational culture, enabling us to collect and analyze data in real-time to inform decision-making and improve efficiency. By leveraging IoT devices and sensors, we can create connected and responsive environments that enhance employee productivity and satisfaction."

David smiled at her contribution. "Exactly, Lisa. As we look ahead, it's essential to embrace emerging technologies in a way that aligns with our cultural values and goals. By staying informed, adaptive, and proactive, we can harness the full potential of technology to drive positive change and innovation within the organization."

He moved on to the next point. "However, with these opportunities come challenges, such as cybersecurity risks, privacy concerns, and the need for upskilling and reskilling our workforce. It's essential to address these challenges proactively and implement strategies and practices that support the responsible adoption and integration of emerging technologies into our organizational culture."

Mark, the head of engineering, spoke up. "How can we stay

ahead of the curve and anticipate future trends in technology and culture?"

"We can stay ahead of the curve by fostering a culture of curiosity, learning, and innovation within the organization," David replied. "By encouraging experimentation, embracing failure as a learning opportunity, and providing opportunities for continuous learning and development, we can empower employees to explore new technologies and ideas and drive organizational success in the digital age."

Sarah stood up, feeling a sense of excitement and possibility. "Thank you, David. The future of technology holds immense promise for transforming our organizational culture and driving innovation and growth. Let's commit to embracing these future trends in a way that fosters creativity, collaboration, and inclusion within the organization."

With their commitment to anticipating future trends in technology and culture, the leadership team of Innovatech felt empowered to navigate the complexities of the digital age and drive positive change within the organization. David felt a renewed sense of purpose and excitement as they continued to explore new ways to enhance organizational culture in the era of rapid technological advancement.

10

Chapter 10: Case Studies and Best Practices

Learning from Successful Organizations

In the vibrant conference room of Innovatech, the leadership team gathered to explore case studies and best practices from successful organizations. Sarah Mitchell, the CEO, understood the value of learning from others to drive continuous improvement within their own organization.

"Good morning, everyone," she greeted, her voice filled with enthusiasm. "Today, we're delving into case studies and best practices from successful organizations, aiming to glean insights and inspiration to enhance our own organizational culture. By studying the successes of others, we can identify strategies and approaches that align with our values and goals."

The team nodded in agreement, eager to dive into the discussion.

Sarah clicked the remote, and a slide titled "Learning from Successful Organizations" appeared on the screen, showcasing

CHAPTER 10: CASE STUDIES AND BEST PRACTICES

logos of renowned companies known for their exceptional cultures.

"Let's start by examining the case of Company X," she began. "Known for its strong culture of innovation and employee empowerment, Company X has achieved remarkable success by fostering a workplace where creativity thrives and employees feel valued and supported."

David Lawson, the Chief Technology Officer, leaned forward, intrigued by the example. "What can we learn from Company X's approach to fostering innovation?"

"Company X prioritizes experimentation and risk-taking, encouraging employees to explore new ideas and solutions without fear of failure," Sarah explained. "By creating a culture where innovation is celebrated and supported, they've been able to stay ahead of the curve and drive continuous improvement."

Tom, the HR manager, raised his hand. "How can we apply this approach to our own organization?"

"We can apply this approach by creating a culture that rewards curiosity, experimentation, and learning," Sarah replied. "By providing resources and support for innovation, recognizing and celebrating successes, and fostering a culture of collaboration and knowledge-sharing, we can create an environment where creativity thrives and innovation flourishes."

Lisa, the marketing director, chimed in. "What about Company Y? They're known for their exceptional employee engagement and satisfaction."

Sarah nodded, acknowledging the relevance of the example. "Company Y prioritizes employee well-being and development, offering flexible work arrangements, robust training programs, and opportunities for career advancement. By investing in their employees' growth and success, they've created a culture of loyalty and commitment that drives organizational performance."

David smiled, inspired by the examples shared. "These case studies demonstrate the power of organizational culture in driving success and achieving strategic objectives. By learning from the experiences of others, we can identify opportunities to enhance our own culture and create a workplace where employees thrive and the organization flourishes."

Sarah concluded the discussion with a sense of optimism and determination. "Thank you all for your insights. Let's continue to learn from the successes of others and apply those lessons to drive positive change within our own organization. Together, we can build a culture that inspires excellence and fosters growth for years to come."

With their commitment to learning from successful organizations, the leadership team of Innovatech felt empowered to apply proven strategies and best practices to enhance their own organizational culture. David felt a renewed sense of excitement as they embarked on this journey of continuous improvement and innovation.

Case Study: Culture Transformation in a Start-Up

In the bustling conference room of Innovatech, the leadership team eagerly awaited the exploration of a case study detailing culture transformation in a start-up. Sarah Mitchell, the CEO, knew the valuable insights they could glean from such an example.

"Good morning, everyone," she greeted, her tone filled with anticipation. "Today, we're diving into a case study that examines the journey of a start-up through culture transformation. By delving into their experiences, we can uncover valuable lessons and strategies to guide our own cultural evolution."

The team nodded in agreement, eager to learn from the real-world example.

Sarah clicked the remote, and a slide titled "Case Study: Culture Transformation in a Start-Up" appeared on the screen, featuring a timeline of key milestones in the start-up's journey.

"Let's begin with the story of Start-Up Z," she began. "When Start-Up Z was founded, it had a dynamic and entrepreneurial culture focused on innovation and agility. However, as the company grew, it faced challenges related to communication, alignment, and employee engagement."

David Lawson, the Chief Technology Officer, leaned forward, intrigued by the start-up's journey. "How did Start-Up Z approach their culture transformation?"

"Start-Up Z recognized the need to evolve its culture to support its continued growth and success," Sarah explained. "They began by conducting a comprehensive assessment of their existing culture, identifying strengths, weaknesses, and areas for improvement. This involved gathering feedback from employees, analyzing cultural norms and behaviors, and benchmarking against industry best practices."

Tom, the HR manager, raised his hand. "What were some of the key challenges they faced during the transformation process?"

"Start-Up Z encountered challenges related to resistance to change, communication breakdowns, and maintaining employee morale," Sarah replied. "However, they addressed these challenges by fostering open dialogue, providing regular updates and transparency throughout the process, and involving employees in co-creating the desired culture."

Lisa, the marketing director, chimed in. "How did the culture transformation impact Start-Up Z's performance and growth?"

"The culture transformation had a profound impact on Start-Up Z's performance and growth," Sarah continued. "By aligning their culture with their strategic objectives, they were able to enhance employee engagement, improve communication and collaboration, and drive innovation and productivity. This enabled them to attract top talent, retain key employees, and differentiate themselves in the market."

David smiled, impressed by the start-up's journey of cultural transformation. "What can we learn from Start-Up Z's experience?"

"We can learn the importance of proactively assessing and evolving our culture to support our organizational goals and objectives," Sarah replied. "By fostering a culture of continuous improvement, open communication, and employee empowerment, we can navigate challenges and seize opportunities for growth and success."

Sarah concluded the discussion with a sense of optimism and determination. "Thank you all for your engagement. Let's apply the lessons learned from Start-Up Z's journey to our own cultural evolution. Together, we can build a culture that inspires excellence and drives organizational success."

With their commitment to learning from the case study of Start-Up Z, the leadership team of Innovatech felt empowered to embark on their own journey of cultural transformation. David felt a renewed sense of purpose as they embraced the opportunities ahead and worked towards building a culture that would propel them towards their goals.

CHAPTER 10: CASE STUDIES AND BEST PRACTICES

Lessons from Failed Cultural Initiatives

In the boardroom of Innovatech, the leadership team gathered to dissect the failures of past cultural initiatives. Sarah Mitchell, the CEO, recognized the importance of learning from missteps to avoid repeating them in the future.

"Good morning, everyone," she greeted, her voice tinged with seriousness. "Today, we're delving into the painful but necessary examination of failed cultural initiatives. By understanding where others have stumbled, we can avoid similar pitfalls and pave the way for success in our own cultural endeavors."

The team nodded, acknowledging the importance of this introspection.

Sarah clicked the remote, and a slide titled "Lessons from Failed Cultural Initiatives" appeared on the screen, featuring cautionary tales of cultural missteps.

"Let's begin by examining the case of Corporation Y," she began. "Corporation Y embarked on a cultural transformation journey with the noble intention of fostering innovation and collaboration. However, they encountered challenges related to resistance to change, lack of leadership buy-in, and misalignment between culture and strategy."

David Lawson, the Chief Technology Officer, leaned forward, intrigued by the cautionary tale. "What were some of the key factors that contributed to Corporation Y's failure?"

"Corporation Y underestimated the complexity of cultural change and the importance of leadership buy-in and alignment," Sarah explained. "They failed to engage employees in the process, communicate the rationale behind the cultural initiatives, and address concerns and resistance effectively. As a result, their efforts fell flat, leading to disillusionment and disengagement among employees."

Tom, the HR manager, raised his hand. "How can we apply these lessons to our own cultural initiatives?"

"We can apply these lessons by recognizing the importance of leadership buy-in, clear communication, and employee engagement in driving cultural change," Sarah replied. "By involving employees in the process, providing transparency and support, and aligning our cultural initiatives with our strategic objectives, we can increase the likelihood of success and avoid the pitfalls that Corporation Y encountered."

Lisa, the marketing director, chimed in. "What about Corporation Z? They also experienced challenges with their cultural initiatives."

Sarah nodded, acknowledging the relevance of another cautionary tale. "Corporation Z attempted to implement a top-down cultural change initiative without considering the unique needs and perspectives of their employees. They failed to build trust, solicit feedback, and involve employees in co-creating the desired culture, leading to resistance and ultimately, failure."

David sighed, recognizing the importance of involving employees in the cultural change process. "How can we ensure that our cultural initiatives are inclusive and participatory?"

"We can ensure inclusivity and participation by fostering open dialogue, soliciting feedback, and involving employees in co-creating the desired culture," Sarah concluded. "By empowering employees to contribute to the process, we can build trust, ownership, and commitment to the cultural initiatives, increasing their chances of success and sustainability."

Sarah concluded the discussion with a sense of determination and resolve. "Thank you all for your insights. Let's apply the lessons learned from these failed cultural initiatives to our own endeavors. Together, we can build a culture that inspires excellence and drives organizational success."

With their commitment to learning from failed cultural initiatives, the leadership team of Innovatech felt empowered to avoid common pitfalls and navigate the complexities of cultural change with greater confidence. David felt a renewed sense of determination as they forged ahead, mindful of the lessons learned from the mistakes of others.

Best Practices for Sustainable Culture

In the dynamic conference room of Innovatech, the leadership team eagerly awaited the exploration of best practices for sustainable culture. Sarah Mitchell, the CEO, understood the importance of implementing strategies that would ensure their cultural initiatives endured over time.

"Good morning, everyone," she greeted, her voice filled with enthusiasm. "Today, we're diving into the best practices for building and sustaining a culture that stands the test of time. By embracing these practices, we can create a foundation for long-term success and growth within our organization."

The team nodded in agreement, ready to absorb the wisdom shared.

Sarah clicked the remote, and a slide titled "Best Practices for Sustainable Culture" appeared on the screen, featuring a roadmap for cultivating enduring cultural change.

"Let's start with the first best practice: alignment with core values," she began. "Building a sustainable culture begins with defining and articulating our core values. These values serve as the guiding principles that shape our behaviors, decisions, and interactions within the organization."

David Lawson, the Chief Technology Officer, leaned forward, captivated by the notion. "How can we ensure that our cultural initiatives align with our core values?"

"We can ensure alignment by integrating our core values into every aspect of our organizational practices and processes," Sarah explained. "From hiring and onboarding to performance evaluations and recognition programs, our core values should be embedded into the fabric of our culture, serving as the north star that guides our actions and decisions."

Tom, the HR manager, raised his hand. "What's the next best practice?"

"The next best practice is fostering leadership accountability and role modeling," Sarah continued. "Leadership sets the tone for organizational culture, so it's essential that our leaders embody our core values and behaviors in their actions and decisions. By holding leaders accountable for upholding our cultural standards and providing opportunities for leadership development and coaching, we can ensure that our culture remains strong and resilient."

Lisa, the marketing director, chimed in. "How can we foster accountability among all employees?"

"We can foster accountability by creating transparency and accountability mechanisms, promoting open communication and feedback, and recognizing and rewarding behaviors that exemplify our core values," Sarah replied. "By empowering employees to hold themselves and each other accountable, we create a culture of ownership and responsibility that drives organizational success."

David smiled, impressed by the depth of insight shared. "What's the final best practice?"

"The final best practice is continuous evaluation and adaptation," Sarah concluded. "Building a sustainable culture is an ongoing process that requires regular evaluation, feedback, and adjustment. By soliciting feedback from employees, measuring the impact of our cultural initiatives, and adapting our approach based on insights and data, we can ensure that our culture remains relevant, resilient, and aligned with our organizational goals."

Sarah concluded the discussion with a sense of optimism and determination. "Thank you all for your engagement. Let's embrace these best practices as we continue our journey of cultural evolution. Together, we can build a culture that inspires excellence and drives organizational success for years to come."

With their commitment to implementing best practices for sustainable culture, the leadership team of Innovatech felt empowered to cultivate a workplace culture that would endure and thrive in the face of challenges. David felt a renewed sense of purpose as they embraced the journey ahead, mindful of the importance of building a culture that would stand the test of time.

Adapting Best Practices to Your Organization

In the collaborative atmosphere of Innovatech's conference room, the leadership team prepared to explore the final subpoint: adapting best practices to their organization. Sarah Mitchell, the CEO, recognized the necessity of tailoring strategies to fit their unique context and needs.

"Good morning, everyone," she greeted, her tone reflective. "Today, we're discussing the crucial task of adapting best practices to our organization. While learning from others is valuable, it's equally important to customize strategies to suit our specific culture, goals, and challenges."

The team nodded in agreement, ready to delve into the nuanced process of adaptation.

Sarah clicked the remote, and a slide titled "Adapting Best Practices to Your Organization" appeared on the screen, outlining steps for customizing approaches to fit their context.

"Let's begin with the first step: assessing our current culture and context," she began. "Before we can adapt best practices, we must first understand where we stand. This involves examining our existing culture, values, strengths, and areas for improvement."

David Lawson, the Chief Technology Officer, listened intently, recognizing the importance of this foundational step. "How can we accurately assess our current culture?"

"We can use a variety of methods, including surveys, interviews, focus groups, and cultural assessments," Sarah explained. "By gathering feedback from employees at all levels of the organization, we can gain insights into their perceptions, experiences, and expectations, providing us with a comprehensive understanding of our culture."

Tom, the HR manager, raised his hand. "Once we've assessed our current culture, what's the next step?"

"The next step is identifying best practices that align with our organizational goals and values," Sarah continued. "We must carefully evaluate potential strategies and approaches, considering their relevance, feasibility, and potential impact on our culture and objectives."

Lisa, the marketing director, chimed in. "How do we determine which best practices to prioritize?"

"We can prioritize best practices based on their alignment with our strategic priorities, cultural values, and areas of opportunity," Sarah replied. "We should also consider the unique needs and challenges of our organization, selecting approaches that address our specific context and objectives."

David smiled, recognizing the importance of customization in driving meaningful change. "What's the final step in adapting best practices?"

"The final step is implementing and refining our adapted strategies," Sarah concluded. "We must take a phased approach, piloting new initiatives, gathering feedback, and making adjustments based on insights and results. By continuously iterating and refining our approach, we can ensure that our cultural initiatives are effective, sustainable, and aligned with our organizational goals."

Sarah concluded the discussion with a sense of optimism and determination. "Thank you all for your engagement. Let's apply these principles as we adapt best practices to our organization. Together, we can build a culture that inspires excellence and drives organizational success."

With their commitment to adapting best practices to their organization, the leadership team of Innovatech felt empowered to customize strategies that would resonate with their unique culture and context. David felt a renewed sense of purpose as they embraced the challenge of cultural adaptation, confident in their ability to drive meaningful change within the organization.

Case Studies of Successful Communication Practices

In the vibrant conference room of Innovatech, the leadership team eagerly gathered to explore case studies of successful communication practices from real organizations. Sarah Mitchell, the CEO, understood the power of effective communication in shaping organizational culture and driving success.

"Good morning, everyone," she greeted, her voice filled with enthusiasm. "Today, we're delving into case studies of organizations that have excelled in their communication practices. By learning from their experiences, we can identify strategies to enhance our own communication and strengthen our culture."

The team nodded in agreement, ready to learn from the best.

Sarah clicked the remote, and a slide titled "Case Studies of Successful Communication Practices" appeared on the screen, featuring logos of renowned companies.

"Let's start with the case of Microsoft," she began. "Under the leadership of CEO Satya Nadella, Microsoft transformed its communication culture by fostering a growth mindset and emphasizing empathy, collaboration, and transparency."

David Lawson, the Chief Technology Officer, leaned forward, intrigued by Microsoft's transformation. "How did Nadella achieve this cultural shift?"

"Nadella prioritized open communication and feedback, encouraging employees to share their ideas and concerns," Sarah explained. "He introduced the concept of 'Learn-It-Alls' versus 'Know-It-Alls,' promoting continuous learning and curiosity. Regular town hall meetings, accessible leadership, and transparent communication channels helped break down silos and foster a culture of collaboration."

Tom, the HR manager, raised his hand. "What impact did these changes have on Microsoft's performance?"

"These changes had a profound impact on Microsoft's performance," Sarah replied. "Employee engagement and innovation soared, leading to a resurgence in the company's market position and a significant increase in shareholder value. By fostering a culture of open communication and continuous learning, Microsoft created an environment where employees felt empowered to contribute and innovate."

Lisa, the marketing director, chimed in. "What about Google? They're known for their communication practices as well."

Sarah nodded, acknowledging the relevance of another tech giant. "Google's communication practices are centered around transparency, inclusivity, and data-driven decision-making. The company uses a variety of communication channels, including all-hands meetings, internal forums, and open Q&A sessions with leadership, to ensure that employees are informed and engaged."

David smiled, impressed by Google's approach. "How can we apply these practices to Innovatech?"

"We can apply these practices by fostering a culture of transparency, inclusivity, and data-driven decision-making," Sarah replied. "Regularly communicating our goals, progress, and challenges through town hall meetings, internal forums, and open Q&A sessions can help build trust and engagement among employees. Additionally, creating channels for feedback and collaboration can empower employees to contribute their ideas and insights."

Sarah continued, "Another exemplary case is Zappos, known for its exceptional customer service and unique corporate culture. Zappos prioritizes communication through its 'Culture Book,' where employees share their thoughts and stories about the company's culture. This practice fosters a sense of ownership and connection among employees."

Tom leaned in, fascinated by Zappos' approach. "How does the Culture Book impact employee engagement?"

"The Culture Book creates a sense of community and shared purpose," Sarah explained. "By giving employees a voice and platform to share their experiences, Zappos reinforces its values and strengthens the bond between employees and the organization. This practice has contributed to high levels of employee satisfaction and retention."

Lisa smiled, inspired by the examples shared. "These case studies demonstrate the power of effective communication in shaping organizational culture. By learning from these successful organizations, we can identify strategies to enhance our own communication practices."

Sarah concluded the discussion with a sense of optimism and determination. "Thank you all for your insights. Let's apply these lessons to our own communication practices. Together, we can build a culture that inspires excellence and drives organizational success."

With their commitment to learning from successful communication practices, the leadership team of Innovatech felt empowered to implement strategies that would enhance their communication and strengthen their culture. David felt a renewed sense of excitement as they embraced the journey ahead, confident in their ability to foster a culture of open, transparent, and inclusive communication.

About the Author

Goodson Mumba is a multifaceted individual known for his diverse expertise and prolific contributions across various fields. As an infopreneur, thought leader, and spiritual leader, he has inspired countless individuals through his insightful teachings and impactful writings. Mumba is also an accomplished author, with several notable works to his name, including "Understanding Corporate Worship," "The Years I Spent in a Week," "Management By Harmony," "The CEO's Diary," "Change to Change" and "Creative Thinking for results" His literary works span topics ranging from business management to personal development and spirituality, reflecting his broad range of interests and insights.

With a Master of Business Leadership (MBL) and a Bachelor of Arts in Theology (BTh), Mumba brings a unique blend of business acumen and spiritual wisdom to his work. His educational background is further enriched by a Group Diploma in Management Studies, providing him with a solid foundation in organizational dynamics and leadership principles. Additionally, Mumba holds diplomas in Education Psychology,

Leadership and Management Styles, Organizational Behaviour, Financial Accounting, Economic Growth and Development, and Project Management, showcasing his commitment to continuous learning and professional development.

Mumba's expertise extends beyond traditional academic disciplines, encompassing areas such as Neuro-Linguistic Programming (NLP) and Positive Psychology. His diverse skill set is complemented by a range of certifications, including Creative Problem Solving and Decision Making, Life Coaching Fundamentals and Techniques, Professional Life Coaching, and Performance Management System Design. These certifications reflect Mumba's dedication to equipping himself with the tools and knowledge necessary to empower others and drive positive change.

As an author, Mumba's writings reflect his deep understanding of human nature, organizational dynamics, and spiritual principles. His works offer practical insights, actionable strategies, and inspirational guidance for individuals seeking personal growth, professional success, and spiritual fulfillment. Mumba's holistic approach to life and leadership resonates with readers worldwide, making him a respected figure in both the business and spiritual communities.

Overall, Goodson Mumba's diverse background, extensive knowledge, and profound insights make him a sought-after speaker, mentor, and author. His commitment to excellence, lifelong learning, and service to others continues to inspire individuals to unlock their full potential and lead lives of purpose and significance.

Goodson Mumba is renowned for initiating the concept of Management by Harmony, revolutionizing traditional management practices with a focus on balanced and holistic approaches. He has authored two influential books on this subject: "Introduction to Management by Harmony" and its sequel, "Management by Harmony."

Mumba's work has significantly impacted the field, offering innovative strategies for fostering organizational harmony and efficiency. His contributions continue to shape contemporary management theories and practices.

www.ingramcontent.com/pod-product-compliance
Lightning Source LLC
Chambersburg PA
CBHW071829210526
45479CB00001B/50